16: PERSPECTIVES IN CRITICISM

PERSPECTIVES IN CRITICISM

1: *Elements of Critical Theory*

2: *The Disinherited of Art*

3: *Stream of Consciousness in the Modern Novel*

4: *The Poet in the Poem*

5: *Arthurian Triptych*

6: *The Brazilian Othello of Machado de Assis*

7: *The World of Jean Anouilh*

8: *A New Approach to Joyce*

9: *The Idea of Coleridge's Criticism*

10: *Introduction to the Psychoanalysis of Mallarmé*

11: *This Dark Estate: A Reading of Pope*

12: *The Confucian Odes of Ezra Pound*

13: *The Religious Sonnets of Dylan Thomas*

14: *Interpretations in Shakespeare's Sonnets*

15: *Tennyson's* Maud: *The Biographical Genesis*

16: *Joyce's Benefictions*

Helmut Bonheim

Joyce's Benefictions

88

UNIVERSITY OF CALIFORNIA PRESS
Berkeley and Los Angeles
1964

University of California Press
Berkeley and Los Angeles, California
Cambridge University Press
London, England

LIBRARY OF CONGRESS CATALOG CARD NO. 64-14725
Printed in the United States of America
Designed by Ward Ritchie

Acknowledgments

Professor Stanley Poss of Fresno State College read most of this work in an earlier version, and I am grateful to him for many suggestions. Mrs. Adaline Glasheen also read several chapters and called my attention to various infelicities and blunders. The reader should be especially grateful to my wife, whose patient editing made this study much more readable and clear than it would otherwise have been.

Contents

1. *The Style of a Rebel*   1

2. *Bloom and Some Prototypes*   17

3. *Self and Society: The "os" Motif in* Ulysses   27

4. *The Father in* Finnegans Wake   46

5. *The Transformations of Mark*   58

6. *The King in* Finnegans Wake   73

7. *The* Wake *Pantheon*   86

8. *James Joyce's Epic of Anarchy*   112

9. *A Rebel's Métier: Comedy and Obscurity*   130

Notes   143

1

The Style of a Rebel

JOYCE REBELLED against those systems of civilized life—
family, church, state, and language—to which most
men attach themselves. Yet he too was attached, mor-
bidly attached, to the institutions that obsessed him.
Although many feel such a tension in their own attitudes, few reveal it so dramatically and interestingly as
did Joyce. Over the years his iconoclastic attitudes
seem to have helped suggest techniques to him which
he could apply to his chosen subjects—procedures of
distortion and displacement and fusion—much as the
systematized "topics of invention" provided the renaissance rhetorician with an orderly method of dividing
and developing his subject. Joyce's rejection of authority became part of his method, a trick as well as a feeling, an ingredient of his system for manipulating language as well as a tenet of his beliefs.
    Some of the earliest fictions show rather obviously the
adolescent reflex, the penchant for saying no, for insult-
ing what other men have loved. But in the course of
Joyce's development over four decades this naysaying
attitude became less obvious in this matter, while the
style itself came more and more to convey the old combination of rebelliousness and fascination with the thing
rebelled against; the newly created words reflect a violent rebellion against conventional language and simul-

taneously a fascination with the possibilities that it nevertheless offers.

The outlaw style, then, did not develop all at once. The genre and the themes and the diction of the lyric verse in *Chamber Music* are so conventional that one can hardly believe *Ulysses* and *Finnegans Wake* to be by the same author. The influences that helped form the later books, however, become increasingly difficult to locate, and contribute less to our understanding when they are summarized. The influence of Flaubert on *Dubliners* and of Ibsen on *Exiles* helps us to understand those works more adequately than the influence of Lewis Carroll and the Koran helps us to understand *Finnegans Wake;* Joyce had developed his own genres and themes and, above all, styles. Portmanteau words, contorted syntax, parody, pastiche, montage—all the unconventional methods of dramatic juxtaposition—Joyce led through their paces with increasing ease and freedom, starting from the conventionality of the first poems, down the trimmed and sober garden paths of *Dubliners* to end in the comic jungles of *Finnegans Wake.*

This development in Joyce's art was not paralleled by a similar development in his life. The medical student's roistering companion becomes the paterfamilias who shocked Thomas Wolfe by appearing on the plain of Waterloo with a picnic hamper like any bourgeois tourist; nevertheless the ironic unconventionalities of *Dubliners* became the violently original *Wake.* Joyce had not lost the urge to make the middle classes jump, but the feelings that were expressed in student revels at the Martello Tower with Dr. Gogarty were later channeled into radical, not to say demonic literary experiment.

A warning. Taken too literally, the judgment that Joyce's attitude was largely iconoclastic seems shortsighted and incomplete. Since the attachment was always there as well as the rejection, we should note a few qualifications. Certainly a portrait of Joyce suffer-

2

ing from a manic attachment to the principle of opposition is an oversimplified representation, although it may yet be a representation of *a* truth.

First as to content. Even in *Portrait of the Artist,* conventionally read as the incarnation of Luciferian naysaying, rebelliousness is an adolescent attribute of its adolescent hero. The young artist's reaction to his seeming oppressors is not merely negative. He seeks attitudes and people, perhaps even institutions, with which he can live, which he can accept. Similarly, one glance at Bloom's and Molly's soliloquies reveals that *Ulysses,* enshrined for a time as the work of a nihilistic rebel, contains characters that positively glitter with Joyce's interest and concern for man, as everyday lives portrayed in literature rarely have. We do not need Molly Bloom's Yes, Yes, to decide that *Ulysses* is not the work of a man psychotically devoted to the principle of opposition. *Finnegans Wake,* too, sparkles with a positive Bloomlike fascination with the world, from stones to stars, notwithstanding early comment on the book: "It is a drama terrifically malicious in expression; it flays one contemporary after another; it brings down all façades of learning and worship in one mass of mocked-at debris." [1] This indictment by Louise Bogan is not altogether unjust. Nevertheless the world of *Finnegans Wake* is also elevated to a mythic and epic plane: its characters live not only in the depths of an ignorant and provincial suburb but also on occasion as gods and princes, as spokes in the cycles of cosmic history. They assume a glory in fiction which we would probably not have accorded them in fact.

As to style, Joyce's formidable extravagances show homage to conventional standards of effective English. Even in *Finnegans Wake,* stylistically the most spectacularly unconventional of the major works, Joyce often operates with a syntactical lucidity that is—or should be—the norm of English prose. In this respect Joyce was quite unlike Gertrude Stein or E. E. Cummings, who left individual words much as they found them but altered their arrangement drastically. No prose rhythm is so similar to Joyce's as that of the directions on the tin beside me telling me how to open it and get the tobacco out. Take ten random samplings from *Finnegans Wake* and the chances are that nine will show a strikingly simple syntax—which is not to imply that they will be in the least comprehensible on first acquaintance: "A vagrant need is a flagrant weed"; "We're all found of our anmal matter." This is typical *Wake* speech, although it often looks much more obscure (346:24 f.)

> Vaersegood! Buckle to! Sayyessik, Ballygarry. The fourscore soculums are watchyoumaycodding to cooll the skopgoods blooff. Harkabuddy, feign!

The first impression, that this is gibberish about someone or other calling a scapegoat's bluff, may obscure the fact that it is syntactically simple, that it is rhythmically forceful and clear. Such language exudes the true fluid—nectar or venom—of modern verse: the observation is not disorganized, but is so tersely put, so highly organized, that it escapes us. But something is observed, obviously, and is being treated with flair and originality. If the reader finds this sort of writing at all palatable, he finds it so because of its poetic genius, its fantastic variety and wit, the justice of its extravagances, and the pertinence of its digressions. Rebelliousness sometimes seems a mere herb delicately adjusting the stew.

Nevertheless, the flavor of the unconventional views —of the underdog, the anti-authoritarian, and the rebel —effectively pervades every major work that Joyce concocted over a span of almost forty years. Although at their first meeting he had accused Yeats of having "condescended to make generalisations," he continued to make his own generalizations of an anti-authoritarian kind, especially in the early fiction. In "After the Race," for example, Joyce tells us in his own words that the "cheer of the gratefully oppressed" rang out after the

4

car race. In *Stephen Hero* young Joyce's repugnance for authority is stated with a baldness not nearly so much in evidence later. Stephen's adolescent striving for self-realization is expressed in terms of resisting his superiors:

> In spite of his surroundings Stephen continued his labors of research and all the more ardently since he imagined they had been put under ban.
>
> [*SH* 26 f.] [2]

He feels personally singled out for suppression:

> [Stephen] knew that, under their air of fearful amiableness, the representatives of authority cherished the hope that his unguided nature would bring him into such a lamentable conflict with actuality that they would one day have the pleasure of receiving him officially into some hospital or asylum. [*SH* 159]

Joyce's anti-authoritarian attitude colors the theoretical pronouncements in this book as well as the portrayal of Stephen's personal problems. Stephen professes "scorn for the rabblement and contempt for authority" (*SH* 107); civilization is defined as "the creation of its outlaws" (*SH* 159); and so forth. The indications in *Dubliners* that Joyce shared his countrymen's dislike of the police (*D* 122, 164, 175) are extended in *Stephen Hero:* Madden calls the police "aliens, traitors, oppressors of the people" (*SH* 54).

These pronouncements sound strikingly obvious and propagandistic beside the anti-authoritarian elements in the much more carefully arranged *Portrait*, the subtle perfection of which forbids such crudities. In the maturer work Stephen's rebellions are more skillfully dramatized and woven into the texture of his feelings about becoming mature and independent. Similarly, the sense of rebelliousness pervades *Ulysses* and *Finnegans Wake;* character, situation, and style are all affected; the anti-authoritarian stance becomes a view of man's perennial relations with man, and, in *Finnegans Wake,* a view of history. Thus the suggestion that Joyce's

5

unconventional work not only exploits but also propounds the view of history of the reactionary Giambattista Vico should immediately arouse our suspicions. The intellectual viewpoint backing the styles of *Finnegans Wake* is that of the rebel, even if it is less conventionally expressed than it was in *Dubliners* and in the *Portrait*. At least one theory fundamental to all of Joyce's work runs counter to the Viconian view of history: Joyce's theory concerning the position of authority in human society.

Critics have assumed that, just as the characters of *Ulysses* are reincarnations of certain Homeric prototypes, history repeats itself in *Finnegans Wake* by successive reincarnations of certain roles: tyrant and victim, dismembered god and his successor, writer and reader. In fact, however, these roles overlap and fuse. Monday's slave is Tuesday's tyrant in the cycles of successive generations. The theory of metempsychosis has its political side: every government, as every stage of life, is an interregnum at best, a fleeting and precarious balance between convolutions. The new synthesis does not simply restate the old with wholly new materials, but reformulates the old elements by a cyclical process of rearranging and reassigning the elements that were available all along, much as Joyce makes new words out of old letters.

This cyclical pattern, for instance, underlies the structure of the *Portrait:* the climax or victory with which each chapter ends is seen a few pages later to have been a mockery; Stephen's ego must be built up once more on some new principle. Man's pride in a new stasis or synthesis is sure to be mocked.

Stephen's humiliation in the opening scene of *Ulysses* mocks the brave words that are conventionally emphasized at the end of the *Portrait*. This pendulum principle in the sequences of victory and disappointment is also at work in the oppositions between characters. In *Ulysses* the positioning of the characters is more equivocal: a character may be both insider and outsider, ruler and outlaw. Stephen is Christ to Lynch's Judas, but a Lucifer compared to Christ-like Bloom. Bloom turns into a Zerlina as well as into Don Juan in the Nighttown episode; he is both betrayer and betrayed.

The cycles of *Finnegans Wake* are similarly viewed. The assassin of the old god is found to be the new enemy, the new god; and a new assassin is called for. Yesterday's rebel is today's dictator: iconoclast becomes iconophile. One year's hero is another year's villain. Joyce's portrait of St. Patrick in *Finnegans Wake* provides an instructive example: he is both reformer and rogue, priest and devil. The bellbearing missionary comes to Ireland to usurp the place of the druids in power: "the shining keyman of the wilds of change" becomes in turn the success and power enthroned. Man may start as usurper, as St. "Partnick," but successful usurpation puts him into the position of that which was usurped. This means that latent in oneself are those qualities found particularly abominable in the enemy. Take over the enemy's terrain, and the terrain will reshape you in his image. In *Finnegans Wake* the ecclesiastics established by St. Patrick in Ireland assume the characteristics of the druids they replaced.

Since this role-switching goes on continually, *Finnegans Wake* is less occupied with the old gods and the new than with the switching of power. As one can see by its language as well as by the metamorphoses of its characters, it deals with the *processes* of change as well as with the extremes of a Hegelian thesis and antithesis. Joyce indicates that these reversals of old and new, good and bad, up and down in his work follow an eternal pattern identifiable in the history of man:

> Our social something bowls along bumpily, experiencing a jolting series of prearranged disappointments, down the long lane of (it's as semper as oxhousehumper!) generations, more generations, and still more generations.

7

These "prearranged disappointments" seem inherent in nature and man's ordering of it; at any moment yesterday's painfully established hero may turn out to be today's villain. The angel who sits at God's right hand will shortly perform the act that will establish him forever as the rebellious naysayer. And as is suggested in his appearance as "loose afore" (378:16), before the fall from heaven the devil is incipient in the angel at God's right hand.

A stark opposition of contrary principles is already felt in *Dubliners* and even more in the play *Exiles* (here so stark that it has been felt to mar the naturalistic effect of the drama). *Ulysses* and, even more, *Finnegans Wake* consist of encounters between opposed principles which are often at the same time doubles or twins: Mick and Nick, Castor and Pollux, Romulus and Remus, Hengest and Horsa, Shem and Shaun, Mutt and Jeff. (The twin-rival paradox is perhaps even extended to the author-reader relation when Joyce adopts Baudelaire's indictment of the reader: "Mon semblable! Mon frere!")

Since all of Joyce's works are, as he said of *Dubliners*, chapters in the moral history of his community, the fusion of opposites within a character or a word is not only a political, dramatic, and stylistic device; it is also moral. Not only individual characters are involved in the switching of roles, turning from good into evil or evil into good. Morality itself is relative, depending on the observer's perspective. Good and evil become subjective terms for opposing forces, father against son, idealist against realist, Mutt against Jeff: principles that, seen objectively, are not absolute good and bad, but simply happen to be opposed. In simplest form we have such relativism dramatized in *Dubliners*. The priest in "The Sisters," who seems at first glance an adequate surrogate father to the boy narrator, is gradually revealed a moral and spiritual incompetent. In "Counterparts" a man is bullied by his boss and goes home to bully his son in turn; role-switching in its purest form. In *Ulysses* and

8

Finnegans Wake conventional distinctions between hero and villain are more thoroughly obliterated.

Shifting roles are implicit in the nature of the rebellious artist, who, before he assumes the creativity of the father, must act the delinquent son, smashing the religiously collected treasures of the parental house: mere knickknacks to him. The pleasure of reading Joyce is the pleasure of savoring both roles at once, that of the patricide and of the father, of the iconoclast and of the iconophile.

Joyce's anti-authoritarianism, then, is more than an accompaniment repeatedly plucked in the course of his stories. The theme acts as a dimension of his work, and as a counterpoint to enrich as well as limit the range of other themes. Where another writer (Tolstoy, for instance) would work in terms of a dramatic situation within which any number of characters may move, Joyce's interest in authority often dictates a more rigid frame: a dramatic dualism instead of a world where a multitude of factors are at play. More and more in Joyce's work the material world forms a mere background rather than an active influence on the characters. Against this rather unmoved and unmoving background the repeated encounters take place, usually encounters between two men. On those rare occasions when Joyce presents a trichotomy, a comparatively rudimentary version of the conventional love triangle emerges, for the third person in the alliance is the woman who constitutes the prize for which the men compete: Gretta Conroy in "The Dead," Emma Clery—that is, Ireland herself—in the *Portrait,* Bertha Rowan in *Exiles,* Molly in *Ulysses,* Issy in *Finnegans Wake.* But the active competitors are almost always male: Gabriel Conroy and Michael Furey, Stephen and both the Church (in the person of a young priest) and the Nationalist movement (represented by the peasant Davin), Richard Rowan and Robert Hand, Bloom and Blazes Boylan (and all the other suitors), Shem and

Shaun. Indeed, this dualism is so extreme in *Finnegans Wake* that it amounts to a systematic dichotomization: Lipoleum and Willingdone, Cain and Abel, Castor and Pollux, Guelph and Ghibelline, York and Lancaster, Mick and Nick, Mookse and Gripes, Butt and Taff, Ondt and Gracehoper, Burrus and Caseous, Hengest and Horsa, Peter and Paul, and so on.

But the switching of roles (Michael Furey, Richard Rowan, Stephen, Shem and Shaun, each function both as Christ and as Lucifer) keeps these dichotomies from acting in a reductive, over-simplified way. And the very plenitude of these pairs results in a multivalued view of the world rather than a reduction to the confines of art. Anti-authoritarianism even gives way on occasion to a reveling in the glories of submission and annihilation, as witness Stephen after the religious retreat, Richard Rowan and Robert Hand ("in the very core of my heart I longed to be betrayed by you and by her" [*E* 538]), Bloom in Bella Cohen's brothel, and all the members of Earwicker's family, especially Earwicker in the "Guilty but fellows culpows" section and Anna Livia in her final descent to Dublin Bay. Evil is the outsider's position seen from the insider's place. Oppositions are never total. From *Dubliners* to *Finnegans Wake*, an ever-present irony keeps issues as unclear and as unresolved in Joyce's fictional world as they usually are in the real world itself. In part, this irony operates in the role-switching of which even briefly-portrayed characters like Mr. Duffy and Gabriel Conroy show themselves capable—a capability that defines their essence for us. Their character is a product of a limited but engaging unpredictability.

The reasons for Joyce's anti-authoritarian stance are impossible to determine conclusively. Perhaps the very springs of his art, his sensitivity and poetic genius, generated a loneliness which came to be expressed as a rebellion against the world. Joyce rejects the community, it is true, because it denies rather than stimulates his freedom to cut through received opinion. But the violence of the rejection indicates that his sensitivity is also felt as incompetence: he rejects the community because it is impossible for him to be a satisfactory part of it. Like Stephen Potter's Gamesman, he disguises his incompetence by superiorly dismissing the activity as unsuited to genius.

Loneliness is an occupational disease of genius and it afflicted Joyce with particular force from early youth. The feeling was surely strengthened by the Romantic stance of heroic singleness, the grandeur associated with standing alone, disengaged as a god. If Joyce has a view of society at all, it is a view held from such an Ibsen-like position.

Perhaps objectivity is gained by such a removal from other men. And objectivity means accuracy, truth. On the other hand, the chances for error also increase, since the lonely man—the Bloom, the Stephen—may raise his loneliness from a necessity to a virtue. The remarkably repeated hints of self-consciousness we find in *Dubliners*, the sense in *A Portrait* of seeing things that others do not see, are in all probability autobiographical. And in *A Portrait* we have displayed for us the sense of separateness, the pride of a man who can live without friends—then surely without the support of institutions.

We have indications, then, that rebellion against the institutions of society (the support and favor of fellow men congealed into custom and reliable regulation) which is evident everywhere in Joyce's work was generated by the internal pressure for self-expression more than by the external pressures of society. Some of these external pressures might explain Stephen's passionate resistance to authority. But not altogether. In *Stephen Hero* he feels that "the representatives of authority cherished the hope" that he would one day commit himself to so gross an error as to justify their locking him up. This is paranoia, not the accusation of a corrupt system which one resolves to fight or reform or dynamite or write tirades against.

There was, in fact, nothing abnormally fierce in Joyce's father; compared with his brothers and sisters, Joyce got along with him very well. Nor can we see anything in the Jesuits' treatment of their promising charge that might have elicited a reaction as violent as the books record. And certainly there is no record of Joyce being oppressed by the British Government: although the works represent Stephen's reaction to Ireland's political situation in the most extreme way—"I am the servant of . . . the Imperial British state"—the truth is that Joyce's liberty in Ireland was never infringed upon by England. Many of his contemporaries suffered harsher tyrannies than he did. He was not singled out by the authorities: he singled out himself.

So the rebelliousness is not entirely the result of underprivileged youth or of intolerable oppression. It is the stance that happens to encompass one's situation, one's problem. Early in youth Joyce must have found that he did his best work when he chose to exploit his originality. We see the process in which doing the unusual, the forbidden, becomes the norm to which the Stephen of the autobiographical fragment holds fast: "Stephen continued his labors of research and all the more ardently since he imagined they had been put under ban." Joyce's own opinion of Stephen lurks in "he imagined." The oppression against which Stephen rebels is a fiction, a mere convenience, as Joyce apparently realized, even as an embryonic artist.

Style and Content

Rebelliousness, then, can become a mere mechanism, a gimmick. Despite his remarkable originality, Joyce did not have the inventiveness, or at least so he himself assumed, to permit a novel to blossom from a spot noted on a wall. He needed grist for his mill, and a lot of it.

Perhaps there is not a tree or a stone in *Ulysses* or *Finne-gans Wake* which he did not see or read or hear about. The raw materials which his prodigious memory supplied, his taste and his prejudices put in order. For the imagination, which the romantic in us supposes unfettered, develops not only material but also habitual methods for treating that material. Like an electronic brain, the imagination, instead of being limitless, free, anarchic, tends to work down previously traveled paths. One tool for treating a subject is to deny its dignity and work from there. The mode of approach becomes a system and exercises its own kind of tyranny over its creator, dictating not only what he says but also how he says it. Perhaps that is why we find Joyce's style and his content to be two sides of the same coin. Nonconformity comes to feel comfortable after a while and always yields interesting results, in manner as well as in matter. Iconoclasm is a parasitic mode eternally nourishing. We see its influence not only in the style of the later works. In the other books, too, individualism as a psychological orientation has its political counterpart in anarchy, its religious counterpart in blasphemy and heresy, its aesthetic counterpart in experiment, obscurity, originality.

Within the restricted formula of seeing a philosophy in terms of its biographical genesis, we might well claim that Joyce accepted any one of these "anti" views with as much or as little reason as any other. In part, Joyce's family and church and state constituted scapegoats for his own dis-ease in a conventional, accepting role in his society. Joyce's image of the artist, offstage from his production, paring his fingernails, unconcerned as a god, can be reversed. Its counterimage has as much truth in it: all his life Joyce continues, passionately, to beat the same horse. He seeks both to obliterate and to justify his own aloneness. He seeks to maintain the fiction that he walks alone because, as in the last chapter of the *Portrait*, his society is not fit to associate with him: this in preference to revealing that he follows an inner compulsion, the dictates of a feeling of separateness. But Joyce does not stand unconcerned on the sidelines; he projects his attitudes both by objective statement and by choosing as antagonists characters whom his own peculiar genius, his prodigious limitations, allowed him to illuminate with the harsh searchlights of his point of view.

Joyce is an author of whom it seems particularly reasonable to say that a discussion of his styles is more appropriate to an assessment of what he achieved than is a critique of his ideas. Joyce's manner glitters more than does his matter; the style is more distinctive than the politics. And therefore at first glance his manner is also more important than his thought; it is certainly less derivative and more distinctly *his* contribution.

Yet to claim that Joyce's style determines or dominates his matter is to say that the tail, being a more original creation than the animal itself, swings the monkey. Joyce is not only a literary technician. More likely, matter and manner stand in some vital relation to one another; the two parts of the animal are appropriate to each other: neither is the sole determiner of the other.

Stuart Gilbert and others have made abundantly clear how the changing styles of *Ulysses* are related to what is said. The complex styles of *Finnegans Wake* also have their concomitants in subject matter: the dream language is complex as the view of history is complex; the one is eccentric as is the other, the one is imaginative and disjunctive just as the other is brilliant and puzzling. In other words, the style mirrors qualities of the material it expresses. The material gives birth to an appropriate style, with concomitant vibrance, precision, complexity, variation, drama, conviction.

Of course the convinced Joycean may feel that the technical adventure makes its own way and requires no excuse; it is delightful and rewarding, regardless of its relation to subject matter. Yet it is a fact that a radical departure in technique satisfies only when one feels that the new technique is not gratuitously imposed, but is the inescapable outgrowth, indeed the reciprocal of some radical departures in content. A pointillist painting is more satisfactory to behold if the pointillist really seems to see his world pointillistically, and we can follow the hint by successfully revising our own perceptions in the light of his.

Joyce's style is indeed admirably suited to his central theorem: that the more positive and creative aspects of a civilization are developed by those who, by fighting against society as it is, fight for it, by those who envision the future as substantially different from the present. "Civilization may be said indeed to be the creation of its outlaws . . ." he wrote in *Stephen Hero*.

It seems reasonable that any author who has achieved a convincing, consistent stylistic innovation tends to be an outsider and rebel in his beliefs concerning extra-literary matters as well. Can we imagine that at the bottom of E. E. Cummings' strange typography and unconventional syntax there lies an expression of Senator Goldwater's politics? Or that Gertrude Stein suffered from a wistful longing for life in the feudal style? The mere whimsy to experiment, the will to be different in manner, is likely to be buckled to unconventional or "advanced" ideas about the world. This is a yoking readily discernible in the political heterodoxy of most of the English romantic poets. (Perhaps, by the same token, the *appeal* of the "advanced" style will have its greatest effect on a reader also sympathetic to "advanced" ideas, not on one whose outlook is largely conformist and conventional.)

Not that we can gauge the left-wing tendencies of authors by the rigidity with which they apply the conventional rules for the use of the comma. It would be difficult to make such reductive predictions about style from the views or intentions of the writer. We know, for instance, how much that is unconventional, the view of an outsider, is written in a conventional, insider's mode of discourse. So we cannot say, this man is a revolutionary, he will consequently write like Joyce. We can say, however, that the restless virtuosity of Joyce's styles probably indicates the heterodox thought of their creator, and that the comic effects suggest an artist-comedian who considers himself a little removed and superior to the cosmic circus erected in his work. Certainly the container is somehow intimately related to the thing contained.

The chapters that follow explore this relationship, and show how Joyce's heterodoxies exhibit themselves in some aspects of his major works, *Ulysses* and *Finnegans Wake*. We hardly need to prove that Joyce felt uncomfortable with certain words he also loved—words that denote authority, such as "father" and "king" (this discomfort is known to thousands who have never read a word of these books), but we need to explore some of the ways in which this discomfort governed Joyce's treatment of character and word. The point will not be to prove that certain of Joyce's feelings distorted his work, but to show how these feelings imposed an additional discipline on it and so helped shape the wit and beauty by which Joyce's mature wielding of the language is distinguished. Finally we must see that Joyce's experiments with words led him to more and more unusual manipulations of language, so that his work became (like that of his disciple Samuel Beckett) more removed from reality, more original, more obscure, and more effective in its comedy.

2

Bloom and Some Prototypes

SOMETHING in the word "father" may displease Stephen
Dedalus, yet he seems to find Leopold Bloom a not
wholly unacceptable father-figure. Joyce's readers, too,
generally find Bloom an oddly attractive man and father. In part this must be because Bloom is kind and
other Dubliners (the young men in the hospital scene
are a notable example) are not. His tolerance and sympathy for others deserves our respect. Stephen merely
fits the seaside gulls into his picture of the sea; but
Bloom feeds them Banbury cake, noting how thankless
the gulls are for his efforts. He goes to the hospital because he feels sorry for Mrs. Purefoy. He gives five
shillings at Dignam's funeral to help the dead man's
family; he is concerned about their insurance policy,
so he arranges to meet Martin Cunningham at Barney
Kiernan's pub, where he is set on by the angry Citizen.
He is proud to say in his own defense: "I am doing good
to others" (445); [1] and rare among Dubliners, he is
concerned about the misfortunes of others. He can imagine himself in their shoes: "If we were all suddenly some-
body else" (109).

On the other hand, Bloom looks like no hero in the
usual sense. He has something of virtue, it is true, but
very little of success. He lacks dignity—for all his pru-
dence and solicitude he is a failure, and we can associate him with such a prototype as Moses (198, 714)

only at the risk of a titter. Bloom is a patriarch *manqué*, a cuckold, an outcast; we hardly find him a conventional portrait of the head of a family. How is it possible to respect an ethic of humanitarian solicitude embodied in so ridiculous a representative? How can Stephen prefer ineffective Bloom to the vitality of his own father?

I am not sure Stephen wants another father at all. Bloom wants a son and forces himself on Stephen. But Stephen's integrity can not permit him to become reconciled to paternity in its normal honorable position again. Any adjustment that takes place in *Ulysses* is made possible by Bloom's position not as hierophant and father but as failed father, as archetypal paternal buffoon.

Bloom, then, despite the fact that he is a father, has certain qualities Stephen is able to respect. Bloom expresses, in action as in imagination, a sympathy for others which Stephen rarely exercises, although Stephen sometimes feels such sympathy, agonizingly—in the scene with his sister, for instance. Bloom is a father with virtues, but without an overbearing sovereignty. Insofar as Bloom wants to exert a father's guiding hand, Stephen rejects him too.

We have heard much about Joyce's war with the father. We know that as Stephen rejects his father he rejects not only family ties in general but church and state as well. The rejection tells us something about Stephen as well as about father, church, and state. The extremity of rejection evident in *Ulysses* and in *A Portrait* indicates its personal importance for Stephen. To judge from all available evidence, the church did not treat Joyce badly, and although the Jesuit life was offensive to him, Joyce said he had not been badly treated by the Jesuits. If we have a look at Joyce's father to find out what ogre might be at the source of all this fervor, we only draw a blank. Stephen's father is a literary construction, suggested by the father of the poet Mangan more than by Joyce's own father.[2] The substitution is interesting, considering how Joyce shocked his fellow Dubliners by putting into his books the names of real people, actual streets, shops, monuments, politicians. But in matters of authority Joyce chose to alter his experience, distorting it in a particular direction. Apparently a special effect was wanted. We find that the war with the father was a device rather than a simple reporting of experience, a result rather than a cause. If it had an objective basis in life, that basis was much magnified in the work.

What, then, impelled Joyce to the violent rejection of father, church, and State? Perhaps the artist in him valued the neatness that a definable cause helped impose on the story of a violent and seemingly disorderly growth. Surely Joyce knew that a clear cause forms and intensifies a writer's style. But Stephen's explosion against authority is also an attempt to define himself. Rejection is a transaction between rejector and rejected; we may ask, what is the profit of the transaction? We see in *A Portrait* and in *Ulysses* that to withdraw esteem from the gods is to invest in oneself. Stephen is less inspired by an animus against the *status quo* or an impersonal love of justice than by an image of himself as crusader against injustice. He is not impelled by such feelings as love of the great Parnell, ruined by the church; he focuses on the rejecting self rather than on the external threat he means to nullify. He does not say so much "you are unworthy of service," but "I will not serve." Stephen means to rescind the law only insofar as it applies to himself. Like the devil, Stephen is out to serve his own pride. Denying virtue to authority, making it blacker than the models he began to copy and insult, Stephen seeks and claims virtue for himself.

Stephen's "non serviam" is the devil's own rejection of authority; like the "dog sage" (512) Antisthenes, Stephen adheres to a creed of refusing allegiance to family, church, and state—in favor of some personal gain. We need to remind ourselves that according to the Cynic creed to which Stephen was sympathetic, this

19

gain was virtue; that the creed of the school of Antisthenes, the Cynics (which means *doglike*), was that
"virtue is the highest good," a statement clipped and
slightly trimmed from the ethics of Socrates. And this
belief in striving toward virtue is to be placed on a level
of importance with Stephen's aesthetic preoccupations.
But Stephen's conception of virtue is one that even he
finds inadequate. For the space of a few hours, at least,
Bloom, failure and outcast though he is, has something
Stephen has not, something Stephen values.

Such an unheroic father without the father's cus-
tomary power and yet possessing some other appeal is
not an abnormal figure in modern literature. Jane Austen's Mr. Bennet is famous for his indifference to his
responsibilities and for his ineffectiveness, matched only
by the incompetence of Mr. Woodhouse, the father of
Emma. Dickens' Joe Gargery, albeit not a father, is
another character in the father's position who looks immediately more sympathetic than does his tyrannical
wife. Fielding's Parson Adams has only a little more
authority than does Joe Gargery, although he, at least,
lays claim to a good deal of power in the immediate
concerns of his family. Bloom, then, is not the first
father-figure to show himself as rather less than heroic.[3]

Certainly a father much stronger than Bloom, like
Richardson's Mr. Harlowe, Dickens' Mr. Boffin in *Our
Mutual Friend,* or the father in Celine's *Death on the
Installment Plan,* loses our respect the more he exercises
his authority, and actually fails as a father as well.
Richardson tested the morality of his day—that a father
is to be obeyed—with a bigoted and disagreeable father.
As a result we find it difficult to accept Richardson's
moral: obedience to the father. Dickens' and Celine's
fathers, moreover, are not even designed to elicit our
wondering admiration; they belong rather with the de-
liberate attacks: Samuel Butler's Theodore Pontifex in
The Way of All Flesh and D. H. Lawrence's Walter
Morel in *Sons and Lovers.* By contrast a Bloom-like in-

effectual such as Parson Adams wins our esteem, whether we find him in a ditch or in Mrs. Slipslop's bed. Does Bloom descend much below this? And Goldsmith's Vicar, emerging unscathed from an extensive series of remarkable failures, is, like Bloom, a not untypical middle-class father, charming in his essential incompetence. Like Bloom, he prefers using stealth to exercising his rightful authority, upsetting his daughters' pot of face-wash when he cannot otherwise convince them to renounce their Sunday morning cosmetic.

How is it that these men—Parson Adams, Bloom, and the others—who seem to be failures as father-figures, nevertheless succeed in gaining our affection? And how is it possible that Richardson's Mr. Harlowe loses our esteem by the exercise of the very rights that have been thought inherent in his position?

Perhaps literature is inherently anarchic, or at least destructive and mythoclastic; the father in the modern novel has lost ground where he exerts his full authority, just as political and social authoritarianism has lost prestige in bourgeois literature. Concomitantly then, we might judge the authoritarianism of an author by charting his use of fathers. Perhaps such a process is not applicable to all the fathers mentioned above. But surely Bloom's failures are an index to a number of his author's attitudes; insofar as Bloom is a parent, it is only as parent without authority that he is acceptable.

Bloom's lack of heroism may be considered virtually inevitable in the light of what has happened to the father in modern literature. Even in Shakespeare the authority of the father cannot be taken for granted, as a look at the plays where fathers take a significant role will show. Where the father claims too much authority disaster results (*King Lear, Romeo and Juliet*); we accept the father where he is dead (*Hamlet*) or markedly permissive (*Henry IV*). In some eighteenth-century novels the position of the father is a little more secure than it was before and after. The father, although often ineffectual, is at least of some slight use in maintaining order and influencing events. By way of contrast, the father has appeared at other times and places as a mere vestigial organ of an earlier concept of the family. It is remarkable, for instance, how the old men of Restoration comedy are invariably out of it altogether, exiles from the center of their society, obstacles to the success of the young. Yet the gain in the position of the father in the eighteenth century, contemporaneous with a greater belief in the classical virtues of control and discipline, was temporary and not overwhelming. Both the Restoration comedy and the comedy of Goldsmith used the same convention of Plautine comedy: the father is outwitted so that the young may establish themselves.

Elizabeth Mignon has shown the marked degree to which Restoration dramatists were devoted to showing old people as undignified and ridiculous, unworthy of respect, and unsuited to the amusements of sophisticated society, and she has shown the unanimity with which this concept is demonstrated by all the restoration writers for the comic stage.[4] On the other hand, Goldsmith always lets the old take a hand in the final union of the young; in their choral capacity, the old bless the marriage which they have helped bring about. Although Mr. Hardcastle's own wife speaks insultingly of his "usual Gothic vivacity" in *She Stoops to Conquer,* he does represent society finally and gives the seal of approval to the younger generation which has outwitted him, as does Sir William Honeywood in *The Good-Natured Man.* But in Mr. Hardcastle we see foreshadowed Bloom's essential paradox: he gains part of his dignity by neglecting to use his rightful authority. He is like the much-maligned Duke in *Measure for Measure:* Mr. Hardcastle's resignation of part of his rights reconciles the young to his position in their world. Congreve, Wycherley, Fielding, Goldsmith, and Sheridan *all* use the trick of disguise and mistaken identity to be resolved in a final recognition scene (cf. Bloom's recognition of his son Rudy in Stephen, and several recognition scenes in *Finnegans Wake*); but in the Restoration comedies this final reconciliation never has full dramatic force because the older generation is excluded from the "comic saturnalia." Such embarrassment about the position of the father has been evident ever since: in the negligent fathers of Jane Austen's novels, for instance, and in Dickens' use of a foster father where he wants to portray a good father.

These examples at least partially represent their own age as well as the feelings of particular authors; and to this extent they are not explicable by the youth of the Restoration dramatists or the conservatism of Goldsmith or the fact of Jane Austen's being a woman or Dickens' mistreatment at his parents' hands. They are part of a larger historical pattern, in which Bloom holds a natural and inevitable position. The ideal of the father-figure as patriarch had been blown to bits long before the time of old Mr. Pontifex in Butler's *The Way of All Flesh*. As feudalism gave way before the bourgeois encroachment and the old political hierarchies lost power and prestige, as the mythoclastic Renaissance shattered religious conformity, so did the father-figure on the level of family give way. D. H. Lawrence has commented on this development: "It seems as if at times man had a frenzy for getting away from any control of any sort. In Europe the old Christianity was the real master. . . . Mastery, kingship, fatherhood had their power destroyed at the time of the Renaissance." [5]

In Bloom this decay of power has come a long way. Bloom's inadequacy and would-be authority mirror Joyce's judgment (or perhaps wish-dream) that the authority of church and state as well as of father are well-nigh exhausted. In fact, Bloom too connects the idea of success in public life with that of success as a father. This connection is illustrated in a number of scenes, perhaps most strikingly in that of his ascension to power before entering Bella Cohen's house. Here he assumes a power over church and state which he never had in reality in his own family, and he assumes that his power in both spheres resides in the sexual function. First he shows his superiority to the church by saying to the Bishop of Down and Connor, "Thanks, somewhat eminent sir." Asked by an archbishop, "Will you to your power cause law and mercy to be executed in all your judgments in Ireland and territories thereunto belonging?" Bloom replies as follows: "(*Placing his right hand on his testicles, swears.*[6]) So may the Creator deal with me. All this I promise to do." And the true power on which his authority rests is emphasized by the celebration in his honor: "*Mirus bazaar fireworks go up from all sides with symbolical phallopyrotechnic designs . . .*" (473). Like Chaucer's Priapus in *The Parliament of Fowls,* he goes "with hys sceptre in honde." Not only does Joyce seem to regard Bloom's sexual organs as the symbols of his authority; here he also lets Bloom fancy himself in a position of greater authority than he ever actually held, thus forcing the analogy between the authority of statesman and father. At the same time he points up the pitiful ridiculousness of Bloom's dream of power.

The principle behind Bloom's attractiveness, that he represents a position without the potency to go with it, is the same principle that makes the constitutional monarchy acceptable to most Englishmen, and surely made it so to Joyce. In both cases the split between the symbolic and the real power reconciles us to the monarch. The king, like the father, is an old lion rendered acceptable because his claws are clipped.

This separation of actual authority from symbolic position is one of the secrets of Bloom's power over us and over Stephen, whereas the consubstantial father is always a threat to the son ("Art thou there, true-penny?"). Bloom *is* acceptable because he is an outcast, because he is a Jew, and so on. As Joyce has it, in one word, we might be put off by his consubstantiality, but can be reconciled to "contransmagnificandjewbangtan- tiality" (39). Bloom is a failure in almost everything, personally and professionally. His essential impotence (". . . uncle said his waterworks were out of order" [355]), like that of Goldsmith's Vicar, is one of the condi- tions of an acceptable modern patriarch.

Joyce, like many of his readers, was pleased to con- sider the family, the church, and the state as mere mech- anisms, directed to the welfare of individuals. When any of these mechanisms tends to interfere, he, like Stephen, invokes his own trinity of "silence, exile and cunning." The artist may be only an unimposing cog in his society, but his importance nevertheless exceeds that of the whole of which he is a part. As Anna Livia puts it, "the park is gracer than the hole." And Joyce puts the same feelings about the sanctity of the individual will into his version of "The Ant and the Grasshopper." Unlike La- Fontaine, he seems to prefer the "gracehoper" or *homo ludens* to that pillar of society, the "ondt." The ondt represents the authoritarian Aquinas, or Shaun, as well as a number of other respectable but authoritarian fig- ures. He does not match the vitality or appeal of the gracehoper.

In *Ulysses* too the pattern of authority is carefully worked out. The older men, particularly, seem to share in the pattern of authority, or lack of it. Mr. Deasy, as old Nestor, gives Stephen unwanted advice, as Bloom does some hours later, and uses his position as a lever to manipulate Stephen. But he does not have the grimly paranoid consistency of Father Dolan (who had pun- ished young Stephen for breaking his own glasses), in whom Joyce's hate for authority comes alive. All the other father-figures in *Ulysses* have a bearing on Ste- phen's relation to Bloom.

Just as he must reject his mother because of her church and his father because of his country, Stephen is naturally prudent enough to reject Bloom's friendly offer of a bed for the night. Stephen knows what his

25

answer must be, since Bloom has already shown himself a little over-paternal. Stephen had sent Buck Mulligan a quotation from Meredith in a telegram that morning: *"The sentimentalist is he who would enjoy without incurring the immense debtorship for a thing done"* (197). That is, if Stephen accepts Bloom's offer, he lays himself open to more obligations and encroachments upon his integrity. Just as he is naturally afraid of "dagger definitions" (184), which restrict freedom as all confinement does, he cannot accept Bloom's offer, and finally, perhaps, cannot accept Bloom at all.

Stephen, like Gawain and other heroes whose power waxes toward midday and wanes toward night, does not have much life left in him in the two chapters in which he appears together with his new friend Bloom. Groggy as he is, Stephen does not say much in all that bulk of conversation with Bloom. But he is not simply tired and shy; as he had explained to Lynch in the *Portrait*, he answers all authoritarians with silence and cunning, and with exile if need be.

3

Self and Society:
The "os" Motif in Ulysses

Bloom's roving consciousness encounters many facets of the world about him on Bloomsday. But his interest in all created things is modified and checked by certain preoccupations with himself. The straying beams of his speculation repeatedly, often unwillingly, draw back to focus on his situation as father and as husband. He is disturbed by his failure in both functions.

It is chiefly to his failure as a father that Bloom cannot reconcile himself. His thoughts continually harp on that theme. Disturbed as he is about Molly's adultery with Boylan, especially as the hour of their meeting draws near, he cannot bring himself to do anything about it.

As the answers to the catechist in the seventeenth chapter tell us, his settled attitude is resignation. He is resigned to Molly's infidelity; when he gets into bed he knows he is not only the last one in a preceding series of lovers but also the first member of a succeeding series of men who will climb into that bed. To this usurpation he appears to be resigned, perhaps peculiarly, disturbingly so, as though it were merely a recurring bad dream, discomforting but not serious. But to his lack of a son Bloom cannot reconcile himself, and the idea of being the last of his line recurs to him all day; he seems able to forget even the adultery of Blazes Boylan and the violence of the anti-Semitic Citizen more easily. Present discomfiture, in fact, is of less consequence to him, it would appear, than that hovering idea: his thwarted ideal of paternity. Probably, as Jane Austen remarked, actions in real life do not disturb men as much as do ideas about action.

> I too, last my race. Milly young student. Well, my fault perhaps. No son. Rudy. Too late now. Or if not? If not? If still?
> He bore no hate.
> Hate. Love. Those are names. Rudy. Soon I am old. [280]

He does not appear to regard his daughter Milly, despite her possible union with Bannon, the "young student," as a substitute for Rudy, the son who died eleven days after birth. He dreams of another son, "like me," to take Rudy's place. He never regards Stephen as his real son, and in the epiphany outside Bella Cohen's when he stands guard over Stephen's body, Stephen is only a surrogate that conjures up an image of Bloom's true, his consubstantial son. Bloom's attachment to Stephen is another trial run—a trial of the idea of paternity, which neither quite fits nor quite displeases.

It might seem that Bloom and Stephen do engage in something like a literal communion; for they drink a cocoa together which Joyce labels a "massproduct," that is, a drink suggesting the ritual wine of the Mass. Yet the communion is incomplete. It may be that, formally at least, either the wafer or the wine of the Mass may singly represent *both* flesh and blood, but it may also be that the communion between Bloom and Stephen in Bloom's kitchen is incomplete in that they drink only cocoa. They drink "in jocoserious silence Epps's massproduct, the creature cocoa" (661) without eating the bread that would represent the host. After all, Stephen is *not* Bloom's flesh-and-blood son. Bloom wants a real son, not an adopted one; he very consciously mixes up the consubstantiality implicit in "bread" with that explicit in "bred": "Bred cast on the waters" (374) returns, thinks he, and his interest in breeding shows itself in: "O tell me where is fancy bread?" (598). Bloom is not Stephen's consubstantial father; he cannot and does not pretend to be. So it would seem that the bread is necessarily absent from the cocoa snack, and that it is significant that Stephen refuses to eat solid food with Bloom in the cabman's shelter (619) just before Bloom is called "Christus" (627), that he lies to Bloom about his own meals, and that Bloom thinks, when he finds that Stephen needs nourishment: "But something substantial he certainly ought to eat . . ." (640). Some of the trappings of the Mass are here. But the substantial, and thus the consubstantial, is never provided.

Bloom, like Stephen, is most interested in this matter of consubstantiality. He himself answers the question, "Tell me where is fancy bread?" Three times he uses the phrase "bred in the bone" to assert that certain traits are inborn, such as Parnell's nobility (634, 639) or his daughter Milly's natural female wiles (365), and he shows that he expects his own traits to be imaged in his progeny. He is surprised to find that neither his own musicality nor that of his wife shows up in Milly: "Milly no taste. Queer because we both I mean" (274).

The contexts of other references to "bone" make clear that Bloom uses the word to signify the essential self, the unchangeable but nevertheless transmissible bolus of characteristics that define the qualities we egoistically believe we must pass on to our progeny. As Buck Mulligan chants in his ballad of Joking Jesus, *What's bred in the bone cannot fail me to fly . . .*" (21). That is, Mulligan is saying, if in fact

I'm the queerest young fellow that ever you heard.
My mother's a jew, my father's a bird. [20]

then I too should be able to spread my wings and fly. Buck Mulligan flaps his arms like wings. It is this belief in the power of inborn traits that Bloom also holds.

Bloom appears to believe that, as the essential self or soul may be passed on to other beings after death, so can this essence be passed on from father to son. The Karmic law that postulates the metempsychosis of the soul after death is thus also applicable to Molly's sexual version of this concept: "met him pike hoses." (*Hosen* is German for trousers.) Not only real death but the symbolic death of the sexual act will release the soul of man to further life, assuming that it has not reached perfection. In this second sense, then, Bloom believes in metempsychosis. He feels some essential in himself which he hopes to transmit to a son. He feels some transmissible reality which is not of the flesh.

Bloom's sense of reality is somewhat akin to Stephen's. He too considers physical life limited, a collection of shadows or transparencies of flesh which he needs to examine for their "bone." Therefore Bloom speaks of the actress, one who portrays a mere image of life, as "snapping at the bone for the shadow" (626). I take him to mean, among other things, that she must try to get at reality in order to fashion a convincing copy of it.

Bloom realizes that he confronts not reality, in the conventional sense, but image or diaphanous material, which is subject to examination for the real thing, the bone of it, up to Stephen's "limit of the diaphane" (38). Bloom is fond of women's drawers not for their own sake but because of what they hide, and examines Gerty's transparent ones with care—his version of Stephen's diaphane. Stephen, walking by the sea, defines his own mission as "Signatures of all things I am here to read, seaspawn and seawrack . . ." (38), and Bloom too recognizes the viability of matter to interpretation in his equivalent walk on the beach: "All these rocks with lines and scars and letters. O, those transparent!" (375), referring both to the beach and to Gerty's drawers. The opposite of this transparency seems to be "bone" in Bloom's view. Thus, having heard the priestly Latin ("Good idea the Latin. Stupefies them"), he feels that when the priest finally gets around to something in English the people are getting the real thing: "English. Throw them the bone" (81), and he does not appear to mean that the priest is now throwing his congregation a worthless appeaser, a satisfying fraud.

Occasionally Bloom uses "bone" in an obscure sense, always connected with an aspect of metempsychosis. A number of times he connects bone with the passing-on of the soul after death, and not only in the normal sense of "bury his bones." For instance: "Bone them young so they metempsychosis" (64) is his comment on the families who enjoy the cruelties of a circus performance. And note the use of "ossifrage" in the following passage:

> The aged sisters draw us into life: we wail, batten, sport, clip, clasp, sunder, dwindle, die: over us dead they bend. First saved from water of old Nile, among bulrushes, a bed of fasciated wattles: at last the cavity of a mountain, an occulted sepulchre amid the conclamation of the hillcat and the ossifrage. And as no man knows the ubicity of his tumulus nor to what processes we shall thereby be ushered nor whether to Tophet or to Edenville in the like way is all hidden when we would backward see from what region of remoteness the whatness of our whoness hath fetched his whenceness.
> [387–388]

This disquisition concerns the mysteries of man's individuality—his source and ultimate destination, set in the terms of Moses' life from the cavity of the womb to the cavernous "tumulus" (burial mound) which will usher us to hell or heaven. The "ossifrage" is not only an osprey, or bone-eater, for *Frage* is German for *question* and *ossi* Latin for *of the bones;* thus this passage also concerns the question of bones, the problem of man's essence. The question of Bloom's failure as a father is

31

a double-pronged one: the uniqueness of the Bloom soul may be granted further life in a later generation either by metempsychosis or by "met him pike hoses."

The "ossifrage" in this crucial passage may lead us further to another curious crux in the episode in the Ormond Hotel bar; here the "os" pattern seems to be broken down into its more restricted components. Lenehan is leaning around the glass dome covering the sandwiches on the bar, flirting with Miss Kennedy:

> No glance of Kennedy rewarding him he yet made overtures. To mind her stops. To read only the black ones: round o and crooked ess.
>
> Jingle jaunty jingle.
>
> Girlgold she read and did not glance. Take no notice. She took no notice while he read by rote a solfa fable for her, plappering flatly:
>
> — Ah fox met ah stork. Said thee fox to thee stork: Will you put your bill down inn my throat and pull upp ah bone? [258]

Here Lenehan is playing the "won't you come into my parlor said the spider to the fly" game, while the jingle of Blazes Boylan is heard in the distance. "Round o and crooked ess" suggests that Lenehan, who is fat, is twisting himself around the sandwich bell. But it seems possible that *o* and *s* also spell *os*, or *bone*, the last word in Lenehan's fable. And this possibility is confirmed in subsequent scenes where *o* and *s* are again used contiguously. In *Finnegans Wake* we find that *us* sometimes turns into *os*, a kind of alternate Everyman (53:4, 378:26, 408:19).

Finally each of these two letters also assumes a separate identity, which Joyce subsequently exploits. "Crooked ess" represents society as "round o" represents individual freedom or the sum total of the individual's instinctive passions and natural inclinations. This trope plays a part in the whole complex of dichotomies and syntheses centering on the power of the family at the personal level, the church at the religious, and the state at the political level; the identities represented by *o* and *s* are vitally connected with the patterns of authority in *Ulysses*. The paternal authority at the level of the family group (s) which must come to terms with those ruled (o) is an equivalent to the hegemony of externally imposed restrictions (s) that Joyce (o) sees operative in Dublin—that restriction that has engendered in the wills of its citizens the paralysis that Joyce had examined in *Dubliners*.

The situation of Gerty MacDowell reveals Joyce's concern with society (s) in relation to the individual (o) in fairly clear terms. Gerty sits on a rock during the part of the chapter that is seen through her cheap and cloying, dramatic style. Then Bloom's point of view takes over at the moment of her getting up to leave. Of course the surprise is that, attractive as she seems, a few steps show that she is lame and that she had not moved on several earlier provocations so that she might conceal her limitation from voyeur-Bloom. And suddenly all her complaints about external restrictions are thrown retrospectively into irony, for it is her own limitation that is far more important.

> She walked with a certain quiet dignity character-
> istic of her but with care and very slowly because,
> because Gerty MacDowell was . . .
>
> Tight boots? No. She's lame! O!
>
> Mr. Bloom watched her as she limped away.
> [361]

Whether we have in Gerty's lameness a corruption of "bone" in more than one sense of the word I am not quite certain. But surely she does show a mistaken notion of her true position in thinking that her problems are due to conditions outside of herself. She mourns that an admirer no longer comes by her window, supposedly because his father is making him stay in; and she chafes against the restrictions of "Society with a big ess" (358) as she calls it, when in fact her own limitations are much more serious.

33

The succeeding paragraphs which describe the bazaar fireworks include a group of remarkable juxtapositions of o and s, as do other sections of the book. "O so lovely! O so soft, sweet, soft!" (360). In five lines capital O appears six times, as the exclamation of delight at the Roman candle—part of the display of fireworks seen that evening from the beach. Now the Roman candle parallels the phallic tumescence and detumescence in this chapter's style and matter. (Bloom speaks of his sexuality: "My fireworks. Up like a rocket, down like a stick" [364].) In the context, all these O's are hardly justified merely by the immaturity of style. Attention to the significance of the "O" has also been aroused by Gerty's reference to "Society with a big ess" and the "round o and crooked ess' in the earlier Ormond bar scene. But perhaps we do not comprehend the full use of this symbol until we hear Virag Lipoti's speech to Bloom: "Women undoing with sweet pudor her belt of rushrope, offers her allmoist yoni to man's lingam" (508).

Here the female organs are twice explicitly referred to as yonic (referring to O or zero). Woman is not only associated with her place in the concept of humors (she is theoretically hot and moist, as we always note in descriptions of Molly). We also remember the pun in Hamlet's use of "nunnery" as "brothel" and his reply to Ophelia's "Nothing": "That's a fair thought to lie between maids' legs" (Act III, scene ii).

Other references to woman as "O gluepot" (418; cf. "Muss his mother was a gluepot" in *Finnegans Wake*, 329:8) or the apposition of "O" to sexual passion— "Madden's a maddening back. O, lust, our refuge and our strength" (419)—point up the significance of "nothing." Both ends of the body may be indicated, as in, "O, her mouth in the dark!" (364) or the resolution to go to the brothel expressed as: "Au reservoir, Mossoo. Tanks you" (418) ("Au revoir, monsieur"). Even one of the words of the sea, "our great sweet mother," is "ooos" (50), and Molly is designated by an "O" in the answer

34

to the last question of chapter 17: "Where?" (This final "O" has been somehow omitted in the Modern Library edition.) In *Finnegans Wake* Joyce came to exploit this designation much more thoroughly. A rough count shows well over two hundred instances.

The mystery of female hollowness is also expressed in "His lips lipped and mouthed fleshless lips of air: mouth to her womb. Oomb, allwombing tomb" (48). This passage urges the similarity of womb and tomb to each other and to mouth, the same pattern exploited in the passage about Moses already cited. The cave image in that section is also suggested earlier in Bloom's vision of the Turkish veil, or yashmak, which he compares to the sheet under which Molly hid that morning (64): "Her eyes over the sheet, a yashmak. Find the way in. A cave. No admittance except on business" (277). (We remember here that Boylan is Molly's business manager.)

Just as Hamlet's "nunnery" is an intriguing pun since it involves the extremes of chastity and promiscuity, Bloom is intrigued by the information that a nun invented barbed wire, as he is with all evidence of the female's conflicting impulses of welcome and rejection. And the idea of women as natural instinctual organisms occupies Bloom's mind all day as he muses on their yonic functions. When he says "Of course they understand birds, animals, babies. In their line" (365), he practically sums up Schopenhauer's view of the womanly genius. He is struck by the instinctual, natural, self-regarding, attracting, and undisciplined opportunism of his wife and daughter. ("Nature woman . . ." [280].) He seems to echo Joyce's respect for woman's instinctual wisdom when he wonders if Gerty recognized his onanism on the beach:

> Did she know what I? Course. Like a cat sitting beyond a dog's jump. Women never meet one like that Wilkins in the high school drawing a picture of Venus with all his belongings on show. Call that innocence? Poor idiot! His wife has her work cut

out for her. Never see them sit on a bench marked *Wet Paint*. Eyes all over them. Look under the bed for what's not there. Longing to get the fright of their lives. Sharp as needles they are. When I said to Molly the man at the corner of Cuffe street was goodlooking, thought she might like, twigged at once he had a false arm. Had too. Where do they get that? Typist going up Roger Greene's stairs two at a time to show her understandings. Handed down from father to mother to daughter, I mean. Bred in the bone.   [365]

Of course this expression is not an isolated example of Bloom's view. There are many more or less intellectual men in *Ulysses*. But even the most intellectual of the ladies, Gerty MacDowell and Dilly Dedalus perhaps, are associated with the passional waters of the sea: Gerty on the beach when she displays her underwear for Bloom, and Dilly when she appears to Stephen, sea-like and green as the drowning Ophelia. And we remember Stephen conjuring up the ghost of his mother's wasted body:

She is drowning. Agenbite. Save her. Agenbite. All against us. She will drown me with her, eyes and hair. Lank coils of seaweed hair around me, my heart, my soul. Salt green death.
We.
Agenbite of inwit. Inwit's agenbite.
Misery! Misery!   [240]

The controls that Stephen wants to escape are here represented by the force of sympathy he knows to be due to his family, the needs of which Dilly eloquently represents. But Stephen has his own way of posing the problem of external discipline to himself. The trope of "round o and crooked ess" has its counterpart in his psyche too.

We see Stephen struggling to define the exact relation of the fifth of a scale to the basic or tonic note of the key. After he has pondered over the problem awhile, standing at the pianola repeating a "series of empty fifths" (492), he formulates his idea, despite the interruption of Lynch's cap: "The reason is because the fundamental and the dominant are separated by the greatest possible interval which . . . is the greatest possible ellipse. Consistent with. The ultimate return. The octave" (494).

A number of hints are given the reader for the elucidation of this passage. Lynch's cap had just said: "Extremes meet. Death is the highest form of life. Bah!" (493); and we recognize the concept first stated explicitly by Stephen in the library with a quotation from Maeterlinck: "*If Socrates leave his house today he will find the sage seated on his doorsteps. If Judas go forth tonight it is to Judas his steps will tend*" (210). Bloom echoes the idea a number of times, as in: "So it returns. Think you're escaping and run into yourself. Longest way round is the shortest way home" (370). Stephen explains his own view of the octave as follows: "What went forth to the ends of the world to traverse not itself. God, the sun, Shakespeare, a commercial traveller, having itself traversed in reality itself, becomes that self" (494). What appears to be happening is that the scale ascends from the fundamental (the aboriginal self) through the dominant (the world), back to the ultimate harmony of the octave (the expanded, completed, integrated self), which is the echo and image of the fundamental.

Philip Drunk, who appears to Stephen's imagination with his Siamese twin, Philip Sober ("two Oxford dons with lawnmowers . . . masked with Mathew Arnold's face"), hints at this similarity between the musical scale and man in conjunction with other men. He makes fun of Mr. Deasy's proud assertion of financial independence ("*I paid my way*" [31]), and hints at the communal love of "agape."

(*Impatiently.*)Ah, bosh, man. Go to hell! I paid my

way. If I could only find out about octaves. Re-
duplication of personality. Who was it told me his
name? (*His lawnmower begins to purr.*) Aha, yes.
Zoe mou sas agapo. Have a notion I was here before. [507]

Stephen had finished his explanation of this completed
octave chord, musical and psychological, with: "Self
which it itself was ineluctably preconditioned to become. *Ecco!*" (494)

This *Ecco!* is a multiple echo. Stephen has outlined
the course of a man's life (*Ecce Homo*) by showing
the end as an echo of the beginning, and also hinted
that this concept is echoing something else, a technique
that Joyce later expanded into the HCE—"Hush!
Caution! Echoland!" technique of *Finnegans Wake*.
Whether this is the intention of the *Ecco!* or not, Stephen's theory of the "empty fifths" is a curious echo of
the relationship we have already discussed between the
o of the self-regarding passional instinct and the *s* of
dominant society. The interval of the alphabet between
o and s (o [p q r] s) is also a hollow fifth, and what Stephen calls "the structural rhythm" of this particular
relation is revealed as a master-trope of the book. For
o and s together spell os, as Lenehan's fable of the fox
and the stork had suggested. We also note that this fable
about retrieving a bone (o→s = the proper relation of
individual will to external discipline, man to society)
is called a "solfa fable." The "solfa system" is the designation of notes on the scale, of which the basic penta-
chord is "do, re, mi, fa, so"—the last of which, the
dominant in the Ecclesiastical or Gregorian system of
modes, appears to be "os" reversed.

Thus we see that the musical fifth has its counterpart
in an alphabetical fifth,[1] and we discover a number of
further permutations of these schemes. "Blmstup"
(282), for instance, makes sense in its context as "Bloom
stood up" with *o*'s purged. But why are they purged?
Perhaps our conclusion regarding the significance of *o*

leads us to relate "Blmstup" to the resurrection of Laz-
arus and to the reintegration of a passionless soul arising
from the dead.

> The resurrection and the life. Once you are dead
> you are dead. That last day idea. Knocking them
> all up out of their graves. Come forth, Lazarus! And
> he came fifth and lost the job. Get up! Last day!
> Then every fellow mousing around for his liver
> and his lights and the rest of his traps.   [104]

And "Blmstup" may be contrasted to the quite unin-
tegrated Bloom subject to yonic attractions in the
brothel, in front of which he sees himself in a concave
mirror as *"lovelorn longlost lugubru Blooloohoom"*
(426).

❊   ❊   ❊

At first sight this maze of interconnections may seem
farfetched in itself and too inviting to a series of loop-
the-loop parallels that do not serve to illuminate the core
of the book. Yet the hypothesis does work, and the complete chord of integration and salvation implied by both
pentachords, alphabetical and musical, seems to be per-
suasive enough that most critics feel it completed within
the confines of that one day's action, even though they
have worked without the light that this double scheme
may shed. As a matter of fact, I am not quite so certain
that the chord is ever completed within the action of
the day. Perhaps it would be safer to call Stephen's
triumph (or whatever it is that various critics impute to
his achievement via Bloom) something that might happen in the future, rather than any actual movement in
the book. Certainly Stephen's egotism does meet Bloom's
altruism and they become momentarily Blephen and
Stoom (666). But to regard Bloom as a Jesus and Stephen as a Satan who are finally atoned with one another, like any analogy or imposed pattern, may vex as
well as teach us.

Even Stephen, despite his role as Satan, is supplied

39

with, to use his favorite phrase, an "ineluctable modality" of virtue, with the "prevenient grace" that makes it impossible to say that he is *only* Satan or Telemachus, or the force of individualism designated by o, since it is only a guiding insight and not a truth to say that Bloom *is* Jesus, Moses, Elijah, Ulysses, Henry Flower, or the force of altruistic communal discipline, represented by s. All such parallels only work synecdochically or as partial functions of the characters in the novel. And the very incertitude of comparing Bloom to all these heroes of authority should make readers grateful: half-truths are preferable to whole truths because they are not only truer but also more suitable for weaving into a work of fiction. The half-truths of Bloom as father and Stephen as son are preconditions to their inclusion in the book. The result is the complexity that many have deplored without recognizing that Joyce is never half so complex as the real life he means to interpret for us. As I have tried to show, moreover, it is the half-truth in Bloom's multifunctional position as several kinds of father that is a precondition to Stephen's integration through him, and even that integration is nothing to shout about. The critics who think that Stephen and Bloom are safely bedded down in Ithaca by three o'clock of June 17, 1904, cannot rely on much evidence from the book.

If Bloom represented paternity only, and Joyce had said clearly that the aestheticism of a Stephen Dedalus required an anchor in beneficent paternity, we could draw conclusions more easily. But neither Bloom nor Stephen is that simple. Bloom does act somewhat like Don Giovanni in relation to Gerty MacDowell and Martha Clifford, but he is also like Masetto with Molly; he does function as the restrictive embrace of humanity (to Stephen's introversion), but he also acts the introverted exile (in relation to Dublin society). Such a double function is often portmanteaued into a single situation. When he says "My joy is other joy" (277), he reveals his creed of sympathy and outgoingness, but he is also thinking of Blazes Boylan in his wife's bed—of himself as cuckold and exile. The loud and moneyed vulgarity of Blazes Boylan (Miss Douce: "You're the essence of vulgarity" [262]) usurps Bloom's place at 7 Eccles Street just as the loud and moneyed vulgarity of Buck Mulligan usurps Stephen's home in the tower. As a matter of fact *both* Bloom and Stephen are compared to Jesus Christ: ". . . *Christus* or Bloom his name is" (627) makes the one equation clear, while ". . . the other, whose hand by the way was hurt" (633) may well imply the stigmatum Stephen has sustained at the hands of Private Carr's crucifying attack; he is certainly quite clear about considering Lynch his Judas when Lynch leaves him in the street (585), and he calls him that later in conversation with Bloom (599). Bloom and Stephen are also both exiles, both are in mourning that day, both are concerned with their relationship to the dead, both have artistic temperaments ("There's a touch of the artist about old Bloom" [232]), both draw on Shakespeare for a frame of reference (one of Bloom's advertisements: "O tell me where is fancy bread? At Rourke's the baker's, it is said" [598]), both see themselves as Hamlet; both of them are sons, potential fathers, and so forth.

Ulysses seems to support the claims of the individual as opposed to the claims of external discipline, *o* against *s*. But to some extent the movement of the book is also the other way—toward integration with the outward-looking concerns of humanity.

It is true that Stephen, as opposed to Bloom, represents what Lynch calls "pronosophical philotheology" (425)—a pseudoknowledge of forms and forms in self; but Bloom's occupation with himself, his narcissism, has been tempered by a greater sympathy for and interest in phenomena outside himself. "Phenomenon" is one of Bloom's favorite words, whereas Stephen is "Stephanoumenos," the martyr to "entelechtual" preoccupations. Framed in these terms, *Ulysses* is about the reclamation of a potential artist to the Bloom-like concerns of common humanity. To this extent it is the claims of society that Joyce would have us recognize. Thomas Wolfe had little reason to be shocked on seeing his idol Joyce entering the field of Waterloo for a picnic, carrying a hamper and followed by wife and children— this is just what the direction of *Ulysses* indicates.

As a matter of fact, both Bloom and Stephen try to become reconciled with the world, to move from the self outward. Neither Bloom nor Stephen is quite satisfied with his self-regarding activities—not only at the end of the book but from the first. Bloom observes two parts of himself in his morning bath: first his navel (his tie with the past) and then his organ of procreation ("flower of the bath, pray for us" [488]), which is more germane to his concerns (his tie with the future) and like his own name, "limp father of thousands, a languid floating flower" (85). Similarly, Stephen has already had his epiphany on the beach in *The Portrait of the Artist as a Young Man* and resolves on the morning of June 16 to leave the home he shares with Buck Mulligan. The Omphalos tower is not only his home but also the navel, the object of the self-obsessed artist's regard. The turgidly expressed resolution that concludes the earlier book, "I go forth to forge the uncreated conscience of my race," is not dropped but remembered and elaborated in *Ulysses*. Naturally Stephen consciously rejects the melancholy navel-regarding function of the artist, and turns "celtic twilight" into "cultic twalette." He is not to forge his own image, "mirror of mirrors," but the conscience of other men, of his race rather than of himself only. No wonder Bloom and Stephen are both intrigued by and fearful of contamination by their own filth—Stephen evokes the picture of Arius "breathing his last in a Greek watercloset with clotted hinderparts" and Bloom is aware of the same sort of contamination of himself (69) and of the animals he sees on the way to the funeral (96). Joyce certainly knew enough about

Freud to connect artistic production to a fixation on defecation. Stephen in the library trying to turn his ideas into money is a species of Bloom in the outhouse: when Bloom sits on his stool Joyce gives us a snatch from the rhyme, "The king was in his countinghouse, counting out his money" (68). Bloom is painfully aware of his failure with Molly and of the human catachresis that his masturbation implies. Although Stephen and Bloom are partly in love with themselves, an "avarice of the emotions" (203) much akin to incest, both of them also reach outward too and are made aware of the dangers and futility of a man's communing too much with himself. Buck Mulligan, for instance, shows Stephen his contempt for navel-regarding meditations:

> His soul is far away. It is painful perhaps to be awakened from a vision as to be born. Any object, intensely regarded, may be a gate of access to the incorruptible eon of the gods.   [409]

Not only Buck Mulligan, but Bloom too, is aware of the corruption that stems from being pent up with oneself too long: he muses about the gas that corrupting bodies shut up in their coffins must give off:

> . . . they have to bore a hole in the coffins sometimes to let out the bad gas and burn it. Out it rushes: blue. One whiff of that and you're a goner.   [102]

Stephen recognizes that his artistic purposes require that he look outside himself. Even when he has barely met Bloom in the hospital, Stephen already considers his potential achievement as an artist to be a link and gift to other men, at least to those of the past: "I, Bous Stephanoumenos, bullockbefriending bard, am lord and giver of their life" (408).

Stephen knows that rebellion must be tempered with discipline in art as well as in life. Thus one piece of music that Bloom and Stephen both admire, though they do not talk about it together, is Palestrina's "Mass for Pope Marcellus," a work not by a self-regarding artist but one written to order as an example of what church music should be like. Stephen seems to recognize that this work he admires was written without the freedom supposedly necessary to artistic achievement:

> The proud potent titles clanged over Stephen's memory the triumph of their brazen bells: *et unam sanctam catholicam et apostolicam ecclesiam:* the slow growth and change of rite and dogma like his own rare thoughts, a chemistry of stars. Symbol of the apostles in the mass for pope Marcellus, the voices blended, singing alone loud in affirmation: and behind their chant the vigilant angel of the church militant disarmed and menaced her heresiarchs. [22]

Finally, when he is puzzling out the significance of that octave which he hesitates to complete, he thinks of Palestrina again, and recognizes the value of prescribed form: "As a matter of fact it is of no importance whether Benedetto Marcello found it or made it. The rite is the poet's rest" (493).

It may be that such hints as these are altogether negated by other evidence, and that Stephen's attempt at smashing the chandelier with his ashplant is an adamant affirmation of rebellion. But I would prefer to see in this symbolic act the destruction of passion, as symbolized by the brothel. Stephen knows only part of his body: unlike Bloom, he has recognized mainly his navel, tie to the past. The striking at the chandelier with his ashplant symbolizes his movement toward the concerns of Bloom and the willingness to take up the "mystical estate, an apostolic succession" which he calls fatherhood (204).

Finally, perhaps the resolution, as in real life, is never quite accomplished—we achieve a balance rather than a fusion of opposites. It is no wonder that Stephen puts his fulfillment as an artist into the distant future (ten years). Artistic production, like reproduction, is the beginning of death. The consummation that brings peace of any kind is also castration. "The rite is the poet's rest."

Thus it is Bloom's destruction of self, as in his relation to Molly's lovers, and his humanity which may be the *summum bonum* that Bloom confers on his sub-substantial son. It is experience and the stasis of personality, however precarious, which experience brings, that Bloom may confer on Stephen, and it is this stasis that Stephen's Thomistic aesthetic requires of his art. Although he may never achieve it in real life, Stephen sets up the ideal at the end of the library scene, once the literary criticism is over: "Cease to strive" (215) is his version of Eliot's "teach us to sit still." This is the ideal, but there is no reason to believe that Stephen or his creator ever reached it. Bloom and Molly, like Earwicker and Anna Liffey, thrive on their states of flux—it is the Moses and the wandering Jew ("very peripatetic") in Bloom, as well as his fatherhood, that leads Stephen to the promised land.

4

The Father in Finnegans Wake

THE FIGURE of the father in *Finnegans Wake* is a disagreeable but necessary part of society, like a man in the
land of the Amazons. "He calmly extensolies" from the
opening to the closing of the saga, as the sleeping giant
of Dublin extends from his Hill of Howth head to his
Phoenix Park paunch and his Wicklow Hills toes.

It is the fall of the father that underlies *Finnegans
Wake*. His innumerable sins are innumerably recounted;
his guilt includes the sins of all men since the fall of his
great ancestor in the Garden of Eden. Yet Humpty
Dumpty acts the Phoenix. At the end the father revives
—the book concerns his waking as well as his wake. At
the end the Liffey rushes into his old arms in reconciliation, the father is reinstated as one of the keys to creation:

> And it's old and old it's sad and old it's sad and
> weary I go back to you, my cold father, my cold
> mad father . . . and I rush, my only, into your
> arms. [627:36—628:1–4]

Even the most extreme statements concerning the disagreeableness, depravity, and downfall of fathers and
father-figures in *Finnegans Wake* must be seen in the
light of this final return or collapse, for collapse it is, of
the female into the arms of the great sinner. Although
Finnegans Wake must be read as a revolution, it is a

revolution in the sense of turning over, a returning to beginnings. The authority of the father is mocked, and mocked more violently than in *A Portrait* or *Ulysses;* but like Bloom (and unlike Simon Dedalus), Earwicker retains in his humiliations a large measure of lovableness. He is dragged through the mud, but he survives. And somehow, mysteriously, he never quite relinquishes a claim to the dignity of man.

The guilt of the father in most of Joyce's work contrasts with a Rousseauistic conception of youth as innocent. Even Adam and Eve seem to sin in *Finnegans Wake* as the parents of Cain and Abel rather than as the children of God. It is not the children but the old ones who sin and fall in Joyce's world. As we shall see, it is Earwicker the father and God the father who fall in *Finnegans Wake*.[1] The virtue of youth is underlined in the book—Germanized into "Yougendtougend" (247:7). Adam's guilt is associated not so much with disobedience as with fatherhood and age. "Feigenbaumblatt and Father" (150:27) go together. Adam's fig leaf (*Feigenblatt*) is worn *after* the fall, when he has cause to be ashamed of his own God-like procreative potency. It is as fathers that Adam and Earwicker have the tendency to abuse their authority. Fatherhood in *Finnegans Wake* carries with it the onus of age, disagreeableness, incestuous designs on the children, greed, and selfishness. We find tenderness for the mother and the children, but very little for the father.

Joyce's feelings about fathers are particularized in certain father- and authority-figures: King Mark, God, priests, kings, military commanders, and others. But a few notable characteristics may be applicable to fathers in general: their disagreeableness, their regrettable age, their distance from us, their corruption.

The Disagreeable Father

As "The Ballad of Persse O'Reilly" tells of the subject of its derision, the father:

He was one time our King of the Castle
Now he's kicked about like a rotten old parsnip.
[45:7 f.]

The reasons for this irreverence begin to be listed in the following stanza, which shows Persse (an alternate name for Earwicker) as a self-contradictory amalgam of the Protestant god and Earwicker:

He was fafafather of all schemes for to bother us
Slow coaches and immaculate contraceptives for
the populace,
Mare's milk for the sick, seven dry Sundays a week,
Openair love and religion's reform,
(Chorus) And religious reform,
Hideous in form. [45:13–18]

The father is made responsible for a great many troubles indeed. One of his titles is *"Thrust him not"* (104:24). To his sons he is "our awful dad" (136:21). As Hump in "The Mime of Mick, Nick and the Maggies" he is termed "the cause of all our grievances" (220:27), an appropriate title for Joyce's father-figure, for he is made to stand for leadership in a churchly and political as well as in a familial sense. "He'll be the deaf of us, pappap-poppopcuddle" (379:20) we are told; he is a "dragon vicefather" (480:26), a "palsied old priamite" (513:20), a "badfather" known as "Dirty Daddy Pantaloons" (94:33 ff.)—an echo of Lady Morgan's "Dear Dirty Dublin"—and a "bad bold faathern" (565:20), according to his own wife.

The father in *Finnegans Wake* is certainly no god of love. His instrument is fear above all, his voice is one of wind and thunder. The course of *Finnegans Wake* is punctuated by "the thunder of his arafatas" (5:15)—*Our Father* amalgamed with Arafat, the hill east of Mecca. Like God, a father maintains himself with threats, by force: "Housefather calls enthreateningly" (246:6). (HCE's monogram initials the phrase.) Shaun himself extends this adverse judgment of his father to include all fathers: "That is a tiptip tim oldy faher now

48

the man I go in fear of . . . and he could be all your and my das" (481:31 ff.). The father is a "retrospectable fearfurther" (288:n. 7). As HCE himself says in reference to his wife, he is "her chastener ever" (553:1). To be in mortal fear in *Finnegans Wake* is to be "patrified" (87:11). Shaun himself threatens to punish his charges for misbehavior until they "yelp papapardon" (445:17).

It follows that an affection for the father is expressed in *Finnegans Wake* only on the few occasions when the father does not wear this fearful aspect. Sometimes he turns up as a lamb rather than a lion, a "lamdad" (486:1). In this innocuous form the father may be associated with cocoa, the "creature cocoa" with which Bloom and Stephen drink their incomplete communion in *Ulysses*. "Lamfadar's arm it has cocoincidences" (597:1), for instance. At this one point in the work the father is *dear*, with the additionally appropriate suggestions of cocoa and fading. (Fading, a welcome activity of the father, is also remarked in "fadervor" [276:14] and "fader huncher" [333:26].) It is the unmilitant father that is associated with cocoa, as in Joyce's Popocatepetl: "papacocopotl" (294:24)—the footnote, "Grand for blowing off steam when you walk up in the morning," also calling attention to the father's latently volcanic nature. Or cocoa is the name of "my old faher's onkel that was garotted" (467:12 f.). Cocoa suggests communion and sympathy, which we can feel for a lamb, a cripple, or a garrottee. But with the father in full bloom, as fearful authority personified, there is no communion.

The Remoteness of the Father

Alienation from the father is expressed in several other terms. The father is far away, ridiculously old; he is remote and alien enough to be thought a foster parent rather than a real one.

Like God Himself in a godless age, the father in

Finnegans Wake is constantly moving off into the faint distance. Earwicker is called *"His Farther was a Mundzucker"* (71:20), for instance. Repeatedly *far* is insinuated into fatherhood in this manner. The old lecher is a "farfather" (95:20) or a "farfar" (482:27). The father "is a farfar and morefar and a hoar father" (139:5 f.), like "Besterfarther Zeuts, the Aged One" (414:35 f.) (*farfar* and *morfar* equal paternal and maternal grandfather in Swedish). He is a "farther" (213:32, 545:17) in space or in time: *"he was popsoused into the monks of the vatercan . . . a little farther, a little soon"* (339:34 ff.). He is "further" (288:n. 7) or one of "our natal folkfarthers" (281:n. 1) or "gandfarder" (378:25). Joyce suggests that the father may no longer be in heaven at all, he is so remote: "the dear heaven knows, and the farther the from it" (396:22). God's involvement with creation is that of the author of a book, the "Farfassa" (398:15) (*Verfasser:* German for *author*). He has made a world, but after the creation can hardly be said to be either in it or interested in it.

The very age of the father constitutes part of his unpleasantness: he is called the "balder" (331:14) and the "father theobalder" (263:5 f.). Perhaps this last is an echo of the classic of unpleasant fathers in the modern novel, Theobald Pontifex of Butler's *The Way of All Flesh*. Certainly Butler's father is referred to in Joyce's "that old Pantifox" (293:n. 2)—the capital indicates that a proper name is concealed behind this title of Earwicker as voyeur in the park. The father's great age is shown in "hoary frother" (310:35), *"old daddam dombstom"* (346:16), "the Aged One" (414:36), "an old geeser" (65:5), and so forth. The increasing remoteness of the father, like that of the gods, breeds less awe than contempt.

The Foster Father

Alienation from the father is also expressed in the portrayal of the father as a foster parent who misuses his authority. Foster parentage is a form of authority subject to the practice of exploitation, and leads to misuses akin to incest, another of the many crimes the father commits in *Finnegans Wake*.

Stephen's feeling in *A Portrait* and *Ulysses* ("Paternity may be a legal fiction") that he is more like an adopted than a true member of his family finds echoes in the *Finnegans Wake* references to fathers as foster fathers. Earwicker is a "quare old buntz," a "foostherfather" (215:13 f.). We also read of "Poppa Vere Foster" (280:17), "greatgrandgosterfosters" (368:4) and "my fond fosther" (489:13).[2] When we note that the protection an old man gives a young person in *Finnegans Wake* is almost invariably suggestive of some illicit relationship, we realize that foster parentage is not mentioned in *Finnegans Wake* as an altogether benevolent enterprise. The book is dotted with the names of old men who fell in love with young girls: not only HCE himself, but King Mark, Boaz, Swift, Dickens, and Wagner, to name but a few. The aged lover is seen to be a "farfather" (95:20) and decisively rejected. Says a girl to a younger lover about pub-keeping Earwicker: "I'd sooner one precious sip at your pure mountain dew than enrich my acquaintance with that big brewer's belch . . ." (95:24 ff.). As the old man exploits the girl she in turn exploits him—she means "enrich" quite literally. The father's function is to be her "paypaypay" (249:17). The situation is clearly summed up in the story "Take an old geeser who calls on his skirt" (65:5 f.). When the girl has enriched her wardrobe at his expense and "she can buy her Peter Robinson trousseau and cut a dash with Arty, Bert or possibly Charley Chance," she bids the old one "tolloll" with a "you're too dada for me" (65:15 ff.).

As a source of money, Earwicker is a faint relative of King Midas. We have noted Shaun's words about his father: "he could be all your and my das" (481:32 f.), which suggests *Midas* as well as *my dads*. He says "Me das has or oreils" (482:4). That is, Earwicker has golden ears. As the secret-revealing Midas, Earwicker presents himself once as "blabus" (revealing secrets), a relative of "balbulous" (4:30). Blabus' activity is "eltering the suzannes of his nighboors" (552:20). Here he seems to be making the neighboring farmer's daughters into parents (German: *Eltern*), with a suggestion of Susanna and the elders. The conjunction with the famous Balbus, of the old Latin grammar's "Balbus was building a wall," is also appropriate to HCE, the master builder and, like Balbus, a stutterer.

The Degenerate Father

Most figures of authority in *Finnegans Wake* are capable of doing good, but are guilty of abusing their powers. God makes the universe. Good. But then he meddles with it. The father creates children. But the drive that brought about this creation also degenerates into the lechery of "an old geeser" or into incest. Fortunately the eventual death of the father permits a fresh creativity to take the place of the old degenerate one. Thus Earwicker's coffin is "an inversion of a phallopharos, intended to foster wheat crops" (76:34 f.). Death itself is a *"multipopulipater"* (81:5). Earwicker undergoes the ritual dismemberment of a fertility god, he is torn "limb from lamb" (58:7)—both *limb* and *lamb* are multiple religious symbols—by the young girls of the next generation.

Throughout *Finnegans Wake*, from the fifth paragraph on, the potency of father Earwicker is rendered by images of skyscrapers, fireworks (as in *Ulysses*), weapons, and so forth. "We speak of Gun, the farther. And in the locative. Bap! Bap!" (481:19). The "Bap" is an onomatopoeic presentation, like "pop," of the father speaking like a gun. Joyce speaks of "poppa the gun" (331:1). So weapons suggest not only the creative force of sexual potency but also the destructive force of exploitation, of brute force, of might as opposed to right.

The policeman, Long Lally, "guntinued" (67:16) in giving evidence. Even Shem is given to "tarabooming great blunderguns (poh!) about his farfamed fine Poppamore" (173:21 f.), and the four old gospellers like guns for defending the sanctities of the *status quo:* "Guns. Saying never underrupt greatgrandgosterfosters!" (368:4). It makes sense that the father's power is identified with swords as well as with guns (354:30, 379:21, etc.). The decreasing potency of the father in the four successive Viconian ages is expressed with the sword as common denominator: "with Pa's new heft and Papa's new helve he's Papapa's old cutlass Papapapa left us" (136:24 f.).

Joyce seems to suggest a law of degeneration: position and potency tend to be abused, a tendency that both justifies our distrust of power and satisfies some vulgar prurience in us. It fits with this law that the simple creativeness of the ancient heroes gives way to perversion and incest, and that the integrity of priests and fathers must occasionally crack. As Joyce says of Father Michael, "*father* in such virgated contexts is not always that undemonstrative relative . . . who settles our hash bill for us" (115:26 ff.). The father has a more than normal paternal interest in his children.

The height of paternal perversions is explored by Joyce in his little fable of the Roman Honuphrius, whose relations with wife, children, and servants are remarkably involved. Hints of the same are scattered elsewhere in *Finnegans Wake*. The "pater noster" reads "Panther monster" (244:34), reminiscent of Panthera (565:19), the Roman centurion fabled to have been the true father of Jesus Christ. The father is a devouring beast displaying an "eatupus complex" (128:36). The girls in the park with whom Earwicker intends to have or actually has some sort of illicit relationship are certainly split versions of his own daughter Isabel, who is also Isolde in relation to his role as King Mark. When we hear that "a damse wed her farther" (595:6), the talk is of Earwicker and his daughter. Like Honuphrius, Earwicker dreams of misusing his position as a father.

Paternalism

Where benevolent paternalism is suggested in *Finnegans Wake* its choking effect is also insinuated, and its gifts are bitter pills more often than they are candy: "The good fother with the twingling in his eye will always have cakes in his pocket to bethroat us with for our allmichael good . . ." (279:n. 1). There are other references to the "sugar daddy" in the book; clearly the benevolence of the old is intimately linked to a proselytizing or exploiting motive. The gifts of the father are mixed blessings: "Heavysciusgardaddy, parent who offers sweetmeats, will gift uns his Noblett's surprize. With this laudable purpose in loud ability let us be singulfied" (306:3–6). Sweetmeats, gifts, and Nobel prizes sound right enough. But the German *uns* calls attention to the meaning of *gift* where we would expect *give*. *Gift* is German for *poison*. In an earlier message this amphiboly stands forth more clearly: "the devil took our hindmost, gegifting her with his painapple" (246:28 f.). The apple Eve procures by Satan's seeming generosity has an unpleasant taste. As Shaun says of Joyce-like Shem, he "kennot tail a bomb from a painapple" (167:15). The apple, indeed, is as dangerous as a bomb. The exploitation theme in the "gift" passage above is further supported by the words "loud ability." This echoes the *Laudabiliter* which opened the papal bull of Adrian IV to Henry II, inviting him to make Ireland his own—supposedly for religious reasons rather than selfish self-aggrandizement. Thus it would seem that fathers, gods, and popes, like the devil, are incapable of sharing beneficence without also sharing a necessarily concomitant pain—being "singulfied" with the recipient or "communionee." The story of the sugar daddy and his peaches is a parable of imperialism, a

54

giving of gifts for ulterior, that is, essentially nonaltruistic motives. The gift proves to be poison, the apple is a "painapple." Even faith, hope and charity, the most divine of gifts, prove to be "feet, hoof and jarrety" (222:30 f.); they assume the features of Satan.

The Father as Murdered God

It must be clear from a number of the foregoing citations that *god* and *father* are practically inseparable in *Finnegans Wake*. The concepts of creativeness and authority apply almost interchangeably to the one as to the other. A name like "fader huncher" (333:26) has the unmistakable hallmarks of both god—the *Vater unser*—and Earwicker—his hunched back.

But the creativeness and authority of fathers and gods in *Finnegans Wake* is not so striking as another position they hold in common. Both fathers and gods are thoroughly and systematically ridiculed. Both are criticized, rejected. There may be a sort of resurrection hinted at: "Array! Surrection" (593:2 f.). Certainly a resurrection is badly required by the time we reach Book Four. Yet the resurrections of Finnegan from his bier and the Phoenix from its ashes and Earwicker in Book Four (after all, only from his bed) are inconclusive. Strictly speaking, the gods and fathers in the work are reincarnated rather than resurrected. "Pappapassos, Mammamanet" (272:5): the mother remains, the children are left and live on as edited versions of the dead father. But the father is quite decisively killed off; although his pieces are picked up after his dismemberment, he is, as Joyce reminds us a hundred times, a shattered Humpty Dumpty who will not rise again in quite his old form. If there is a constant in *Finnegans Wake*, it is mother rather than father, goddess rather than god; fickleness is a feature of the active, aggressive and mobile male; the female endures, is pitied, survives. With a few exceptions, such as that of the prankquean, the woman is a rather passive agent. She survives, at least for a time. But the father, the villain, cannot be permitted the grace of a natural death.

Joyce goes further in destroying the father. The overthrow or death of the father does not simply happen; it is preordained, necessary. "Pressures be to our hoary frother" (310:35) pray the children of their beer-frothed father. The death of the old creator is a necessary precondition to later existence:

> . . . on the bunk of our breadwinning lies the cropse of our seedfather, a phrase which the establisher of the world by law might pretinately write across the chestfront of all manorwombanborn.
> [55:7–10]

The corpse of the seed gives rise to a new life; the corpse turns to crops. The father's survivors make his coffin a symbol of fertility, a procedure "intended to foster wheat crops" (76:35).

The father, in effect, is a priest-king whose death is required for further life:

> As hollyday in his house so was he priest and king to that; ulvy came, envy saw, ivy conquered. Lou! Lou! They have waved his green boughs o'er him as they have torn him limb from lamb. For his muertification and uxpiration and dumnation and annuhulation. [58:5–9]

The pattern is repeated again and again: here Anna Livia ("ulvy") comes, the conqueror's power over her is envied by others who see it, nature conquers in turn, effecting the priest-king's annihilation. The annual and natural quality of this rite, hinted at in "annuhulation," takes its place as "annua" and "natu" in the hundred-lettered thunderword devoted to the violent demise of the father:

> Pappappapparrassannuaragheallachnatullaghmon-
> ganmacmacmacwhackfalltherdebblenonthedub-
> blandaddydoodled. [332:5 ff.]

With a great deal of "pep for his perdition" (282:3), the

father is done in. When Joyce sends his original yuletide greetings at the end of the school-lesson chapter, he makes quite clear that the parents he addresses are no longer of this world:

> With our best youlldied greedings to Pep and Memmy and the old folkers below and beyant. . . .
>
> [308:17 ff.]

The father has been safely put away.

5

The Transformations of Mark

THE TRISTAN AND ISOLDE story in *Finnegans Wake* provides another instructive example of the directions in which Joyce distorts both the language and the myriad myths and particles of the nightmare of history. The three points of the Tristan love triangle in *Finnegans Wake* are treated in typically Joycean fashion: whereas the two juniors, Tristan and Isolde, are re-modeled into more contemporary heroes, into rainbow girls and the like, Mark is slandered and vilified merci-lessly. Tristan is familiarized as Tristy, naturalized into Treestone, reversed into the armor he wears with Isolde (a "natsirt"), called a tactful lover, and so forth; but King Mark is toppled, besmirched, and hung up by the heels like a modern dictator. As one of the many sur-rogates for the father-king-authoritarian hero HCE, Mark suffers a wide sampling of Joyce's genius for in-sult. For the rebellious young ones over whom he would reign, "He's their mark" (363:15).

But Mark of Cornwall is not the only Mark in *Finne-gans Wake*. The name sometimes refers to Mark Twain, and more frequently to St. Mark, author of the second gospel. In most of St. Mark's appearances in the book he is included in passages in which all four gospelers take part: Matthew, Mark, Luke, and, usually trailing behind a little, John. The members of this quartet usu-ally appear in the order fixed by the combination "Mamalujo," but also in a great variety of other disguises, such as the following:

> Are you meanam Tarpey and Lyons and Gregory? I meyne now, thank all, the four of them, and the roar of them, that draves that stray in the mist and old Johnny MacDougal along with them.

[214:33–215:1]

The evangelist Mark may be more clearly indicated than this, as in "matt your mark, though luked your johl" (245:29 f.). (*Matt* is German for *exhausted* or *dull*; *johlen* is German for *howling* or *hooting*.) Or Mark may turn into "wishmarks" (251:17), "sammarc" (253:12), "Marusias" (256:21), "Markandeyn" (525:28), and so forth. Whenever some version of the word "mark" appears as one of a group of four, we know it concerns the gospeler St. Mark. But Mark steps on stage in other guises, often in other roles. Finn MacCool himself is Mark, since he has King Mark's position in the Irish version of the Tristan and Isolde story, Diarmid and Grainne. Thus the fall of Finnegan, the fall that precedes the great Wake in *Finnegans Wake,* is also the fall of Mark, in his various manifestations, as it is the fall of HCE, Adam, Humpty Dumpty, Parnell, and others.

In a sense all these falling heroes in *Finnegans Wake* are the same hero. As I argued earlier, in altered or attenuated form the heroes fuse with their predecessors and successors, the gods and masters amalgamate with their victims and slaves. Many such associations proliferate in the course of *Finnegans Wake* until almost every amalgamating link is somehow connected to every other to provide an image of all human experience in its odd unity as well as its maddening diversity. Therefore we can explore only a few of Mark's disguises and identities. A thorough investigation might require the inclusion of almost everything in the work, all the parts of which echo and reëcho each other.

Let us see how some of Mark's important disguises are worked out and put to use in the course of the book.

59

When we read, for instance, that "Foremaster's meed [3] will mark tomorrow" (305:31 f.), we know that "mark is Mark, one of the four masters, and that he must occupy the second position in the third footnote at the bottom of the page: "Giglamps, Soapy Geyser, The Smell and Gory Mac Gusty." Similarly, when we read "mark well what I say" (480:11, 565:8), or "mark one autonement" (568:9), or "Bemark you these hangovers" (567:12), we know that reference is made to Mark.

Mark is distinguished from the other gospelers in that his particular mode is light and dark. It is true that light and dark is a fourth dimension applicable to all four gospelers: their abodes are "their fourdimmansions" (367:27). But to be described in terms of light and dark is Mark's peculiar distinction. His is the second position in the "audible-visible-gnosible-edible world" (88:6). He is "murk" in the quartet of Matthew, Mark, Luke, and John: "Mildew, murk, leak and yarn" (598:22). His failure with Isolde is associated with lack of light: "Murk, his vales are darkling. . . . Hairfluke, if he could bad twig her!" (23:23, 25). Indeed, Mark as king has a "vale" before his eyes in his attempts to catch Isolde out in her affair with Tristan; finally he is "undeveiled" (75:5 f.). The "fluke" of seeing the telltale hair gives him grounds for suspecting Isolde's adultery ("Hairfluke" also echoes the German expletive *verflucht*, meaning *accursed*). Perhaps King Mark in his failure to prevent his own cuckoldry resembles Leopold Bloom and *Exiles'* Richard Rowan: like them he advances his own betrayal more knowingly than we might expect of a tragic hero.

Neither in his role as one of the four gospelers—the "four avunculusts" (367:14)—nor as king does Mark get very much respect. Normally he is one of "the grinning statesmen" (272:25), and his "comicsongbook soul" (380:24) is suitable for inclusion in the "senior follies" (397:11) put on by "Mamalujo" (398:4) or "Mamma Lujah" (614:28), the four old men telescoped.

Mark as "Markeehew (399:29) and "Marahah" (554:10) is an object of joking rather than of respect, more derided than any other of the "four ghools" (377:34). As King Mark he is also the butt of merriment and scorn: "A king off duty and a jaw for ever!" (162:35) rather than "a thing of beauty and a joy forever." He is the "goat" (Italian: *becco*) of Tristan and Isolde: "He has becco of wild hindigan. Ho, he hath hornhide!" (403:13 f.). The *becco*, which is also the Italian equivalent of the traditional cuckold's horns, emphasizes Mark's defeat at the hands of Isolde. Elsewhere he is described as "dishorned" (112:22).

It is true that Mark does not only play the dupe. Like his larger self, Earwicker, he can sometimes take up the offensive against his detractors, and on occasion he may be a lively one with women, in relation to whom he is a warrior at the famous "Charge of the Light Brigade":

> . . . a great mark for jinking and junking, up the palposes of womth and wamth, we war, and the charme of their lyse brocade. [348:24]

Here the "lyse brocade" indicates that the lower-case "great mark" refers to Mark of Cornwall, since "leise" in *Finnegans Wake* normally refers to the "Mild und leise" aria of Wagner's "Tristan and Isolde."

But such activity as "jinking and junking" is not normal for Mark. On the whole he is on the defensive, and he comes off badly, apparently insulted for very good reasons. In reading that Mark of Cornwall is duped by Isolde, we also hear how mean he is:

> Lonely went to play your mother, isod? You was wiffriends? Hay, dot's a doll yarn! Mark mean then! [444:34 f.]

We are asked to pity the victim, Isolde, although she does spin Mark a doll yarn (*doll* or *toll* is also German for *mad, extreme*):

> . . . it must have been, faw! a terrible mavrue mavone, to synamite up the old Adam-he-used-to, such a finalley, and that's flat as Tut's fut, for

whowghowho? the poour girl, a lonely peggy,
given the bird, so inseuladed as Crampton's pear-
tree, (she sall eurn bitter bed by thirt sweet of her
face!). . . .   [291:2–6]

In echoes from the "Twelve days of Christmas" we are
asked to pity Isolde, the "lonely peggy" who is at Mark's
mercy. We are reminded that Mark is a seizer and caesar
whom Isolde cannot respect: "The older sisars (Tyrants,
regicide is too good for you!) become unbeurrable from
age . . ." (162:1 f.). But where Mark is the exploited
and weaker creature, he too is due some sympathy, as
in one passage showing him massacred and persecuted:

Ah, now, it was too bad, too bad and stout entirely,
all the missoccurs; and poor Mark or Marcus Bo-
wandcoat, from the brownesberrow in nolands-
land, the poor old chronometer, all persecuted with
ally croaker by everybody, by decree absolute,
through Herrinsilde.   [391:12–16]

Through the recurring themes of violence here—massa-
cre, Bruno of Nola and the allies—there emerges the
primacy of "Herrinsilde." Here Isolde is the master, the
Herrin of the *Insel* (German for *island*), as well as a
herring (Danish: *sild*). Old Mark in his race with Tristan
is a mere "chronometer"; it is his job to "Mark Time's"
(455:30).

The tale of Mark's betrayal is told and retold in
Finnegans Wake, perhaps most characteristically where
the affair is recounted in the manner of "the new world
presses":

. . . the drowning of Pharoah and all his pedes-
trians and they were all completely drowned into
the sea, the red sea, and then poor Merkin Cornyng-
wham, the official out of the castle on pension, when
he was completely drowned off Erin Isles, at that
time, suir knows, in the red sea and a lovely mourning paper and thank God, as Saman said, there were
no more of him. And that now was how it was. The
arzurian deeps o'er his humbodumbones sweeps.

And his widdy the giddy is wreathing her murmoirs as her gracest triput to the Grocery Trader's Manthly. Mind mand gunfree by Gladeys Rayburn! Runtable's Reincorporated. The new world presses. Where the old conk cruised now croons the yunk. Exeunc throw a darras Kram of Llawnroc, ye gink guy, kirked into yord. Enterest attawonder Wehpen, luftcat revol, fairescapading in his natsirt. Tuesy tumbles. And mild aunt Liza is as loose as her neese. Fulfest withim inbrace behent. As gent would deem oncontinent. [387:26–388:5]

In rough translation the passage reads somewhat like this: Pharoah, like Mark, is punished (in each case by natural forces which take revenge on his attempt to press the advantages of his position and his authority too far). Mark of Cornwall is an old man who dies. Thank God, says someone (this someone is also the force of new life, for *Samen* is German for *seed* while *saman* is the original Tungesic form of *shaman,* or *medicine man*). The Arthurian-azure deeps roll over his Humpty-Dumpty bones. And his giddy widow is writing his memoirs as her greatest tribute—for the Grocery Trader's Monthly. "My man gone free" ("My man Godfrey") by Glad Eyes' Rays Burn (Isolde-Isabel-the-Temptresses are often connected with light, an association appropriate to the equation of Mark with the visible world). The round table renewed. A version of the tale as a modern newspaper might retail it: where the old king cruised the young one now croons. (Echo of the recurring rebellion motif. Cf. "Ubipop jay piped, ibipep goes the whistle" [540:14 f.]. That is, where the father sang, the peppy youth now whistles.) Exit through a curtain uncle Marc of Cornwall (written in the mirror style that Tristan himself employed). (*Kram* is German for *old rubbish,* an appellation Mark receives again at 515:3 ["cram"]. The old king is buried in the churchyard. Enter at a window the wonder, the tactful lover (read backward again) with revolver held high, escapading Tristan (natsirt reversed) coming in from the fire escape (echo of Parnell) in his night shirt. Yseut falls. The "Mild und leise" aria sounds. The scene ends with such embracing and passion as a gentleman would think excessive.

In this passage the myth of Mark is performed in modern dress, somewhat as *Ulysses* modernizes its Homeric prototype, imposing onto the grandeur of the classical model the tawdriness of naturalistic detail. The poem that opens the chapter had already presented a similar amalgam of Mark the grand and Mark the mean. There the mixed nature of Mark's royal position and humble function is compressed into *"Wreneagle Almighty"*:

> — *Three quarks for Muster Mark!*
> *Sure he hasn't got much of a bark*
> *And sure any he has it's all beside the mark.*
> *But O, Wreneagle Almighty, wouldn't un be a sky of a lark*
> *To see that old buzzard whooping about for uns shirt in the dark*
> *And he hunting round for uns speckled trousers around by Palmerstown Park?*
> *Hohohoho, moulty Mark!*
> *You're the rummest old rooster ever flopped out of a Noah's ark*
> *And you think you're cock of the wark.*
> *Fowls, up! Tristy's the spry young spark*
> *That'll tread her and wed her and bed her and red her*
> *Without ever winking the tail of a feather*
> *And that's how that chap's going to make his money and mark!*   [383:1–14]

This is not the only passage in which Mark descends from his throne to be identified with birds and other humble animals. We have already seen that "the snuggest spalniel's where the lieon's tame!" (350:30) and that Mark may be regarded as a "grand old greeneyed lobster" (249:3). "Lobster" is a traditional contemptuous term for the English redcoat, and also echoes a famous actor's blunder for Iago's "green-eyed monster." [1] Shakespeare's metaphor for jealousy is, of course, appropriate to King Mark's situation. In the same line "viewmarc" reminds us again of Mark's weakening, his age (French: *vieux*). Later he turns into animal characters out of Lewis Carroll: the "markshaire" (423:3) and the "smark" (601:36). He is one of the "four wethers" (604:34). Sharing the guilt of HCE as he does, as the patriarchal shamanah" (75:14), he becomes the Satanic snake himself, in the context of the epic of Gilgamesh: "an engles to the teeth who, nomened Nash of Girahash, would go anyold where in the weeping world on his mottled belly (the rab, the kreeponskneed!) for milk, music, or married missusses" (75:19–22).

Wherever a lion is mentioned in *Finnegans Wake* it acts as surrogate for Joyce's Mark, which is reasonable enough, since the lion has long been St. Mark's representative in Christian symbolism. Often this representation is made quite clear, as when Mark appears with the other gospelers: "Gregorius, Leo, Vitellius and Macdugalius" (573:8, 28). This animal symbolism must also alert us to some of Mark's less obvious appearances: we read "From Daneland sailed the oxeyed man, now mark well what I say" (480:10 f.). Here we see that the traditional representatives of Luke, the calf or the ox, appear as such in *Finnegans Wake*s the "mark" that follows must be Mark. When Yawn addresses the gospelers, he amalgamates Luke and Mark as "kalblionized" (483:22). (*Kalb* is German for *calf*). The same identification occurs in "Marcus Lyons and Lucas Metcalfe Tarpey" (476:26). Mark dreaming of Isolde is compared to a lion in the zoo in that curious and poetic passage that opens the fourth chapter of Book I:

As the lion in our teargarten remembers the nenu-

phars of his Nile . . . the besieged bedreamt him
. . . of those lililiths undeveiled which had undone
him. . . .   [75:1–6]

The lion in the zoo (German: *Tiergarten*) remembers
the Nile nenuphars (lilies); similarly HCE dreams of
the lilies (girls) in the park who had undone (disrobed,
ruined) him, just as Bloom (another Leo) had en-
visioned various illicit delights. The besieged is Mark
too, for four lines later the dream is said to be of "corn-
gold Ysit," that is, of Isolde. Isolde is called a lily elsewhere (618:4).

If Mark is lion, Isolde is lioness: "the manewanting
human lioness with her dishorned discipular manram"
(112:21 f.). Here the disciple Mark is fused with the
dishorned King Mark.

Mark as dupe and buffoon undergoes other transformations as well: he is not only animalized but feminized, like so many other characters in *Ulysses* and
Finnegans Wake. He is introduced variously as "MAW"
(308:margin), as one of the housebroken "old connubial
men of the sea" (386:4 f.), as one of the "four dear old
heladies" (386:14 f.), and as Snow White's mother-in-
law; he also turns into "the old markiss their besterfar"
(96:5), one of the "dear poor shehusbands" (390:20).
Later he appears again as the cripple and cuptosser
Mrs. Lyons (519:33, 520:13). This feminization of the
hero in contrast to his lionization is a contradiction
for which the reader of *Ulysses* will be prepared; for
Bloom, despite the lion lurking in "Leopold," turns
into a woman several times in the Nighttown episode.

We note that Mark appears more often in the "Lyons"
spelling than in the more normal one. We see him clearly
as "Marcus Lyons" in a number of instances other than
those already cited (384:8, 388:34, 405:4). And King
Mark's wife, Isolde, becomes "my lady of Lyons"
(449:11) when Jaun presents her as his sister. This
spelling may be demanded by an association of Mark

66

with the English "Lyons' Tea House," a linkage we note in the "lion in our teargarten" passage. Mark's heraldic animal is also linked with teashops by the usurper Shem-Tristan, who calls the forces of conventionality and respectability arrayed against him "the teashop lionses of Lumdrum" (177:36 f.). (In reference to the four gospelers London is "Leonden" [541:16].)

If we are entitled to associate Mark with the commercial enterprise of the Lyons' chain of teashops, this association suggests another of his functions in *Finnegans Wake,* another aspect of the indictment to which he is subject in common with HCE. That is, Mark incorporates the Shaunish qualities of HCE himself. As a businessman and foreign invader, he represents an exploiter of Ireland, like pub-owner Earwicker. Mark the lion takes the lion's share of whatever enterprise he participates in: "Longhorns Connacht, stay off my air! You've grabbed the capital and you've had the lion's shire" (528:27 f.).

Mark's business activities bring out the censor and autocrat in him. He demands obedience:

> . . . eliminating ["desultory delinquency" we read at this point in the version of the passage which appeared in *Transition*] from all classes and masses with directly derivative decasualisation: *sigarius* (sic!) *vindicat urbes terrorum* (sicker!): and so, to mark a bank taal she arter, the obedience of the citizens elp the ealth of the ole.   [76:6–9]

Here we see Mark associated with the conquering capitalist or banker smoking the "sigarius" into which the "securus" in Dublin's motto has turned. To him individual liberty is naturally secondary to the health of the whole society (or his own): he needs obedient and "decasualized" citizens. Mark at times can be an "old determined despot" (386:18) who rules and is ruled "by decree absolute" (390:33, 391:16).

Once we see the association of Mark with business we can better understand the curious passage on page 403 (part of which is entitled "Mark as capsules") in which Jugurtha, with "becco of wild hindigan," appears. As Campbell and Robinson explain,[2] Jugurtha predicted that the commercialism of imperial Rome would bring about its fall. Both accuser and accused show Mark's characteristics: Mark is a cuckold (he has a "becco"), is identified with Finnegan (the "wild hindegan"), and bears the features of commercial man. Indeed, we find some pages later, in the following chapter, that Mark, like Cain, with whom he is elsewhere associated (47:29, 491:16), is a marked man; and one of his marks is money: "He's a markt man" (442:18). (German *Markt:* market.) And one of Mark's many aliases is reminiscent of Shaw's munitions magnate, Undershaft: "S. Mark Underloop" (569:5). If he is a businessman, Mark is not a respectable one: "Lowe, you blondy liar, Gob scene you in the narked place" (34:9 f.). A *nark,* implied here as well as *market,* is Romany (which Joyce played with in *Ulysses*) for a *betrayer* or *police spy;* "Lowe" indicates the heraldic lion of St. Mark (German: *Löwe*). Mark is labeled *nark* a number of times (368:22, 369:20, 581:8, 621:20, and elsewhere). This insult tallies with his appellation as "Mr Sneakers" (618:5 f.).

Mark is subject to Jugurtha's judgment in another sense. He is a Roman sort of king, we find: "properly SPQeaRking Mark Time's Finist Joke" (455:29 f.). Properly speaking, the "queer" SPQR on his banner stands for the "small profits, quick returns" of the businessman as well as for *Senatus Populusque Romanus,* the body that gave way to the Eastern hordes of "wild hindigans." Later in the same chapter the ungenerous exploiting character of Mark is emphasized: "Mark my use of you, cog!" (464:3 f.). He is a "tightmark" (262:n. 1), and his high station is made possible only by the labor of others. It may be that Mark is the sort of personage we meet continually in the heroic statuary of civic parks, but it is the sweat of other men that make up his monument: "the palmsweat on high is the mark of your manument" (25:15 f.). Even Mark's alter ego, Shaun, accuses him indirectly of colonialist exploitation. When Shaun wants to speak of Shem's exile, he calls it "his coglional expancian" (488:31 f.). Colonialism is the lion's, that is, Mark's sort of activity. The fact that he wants the "lion's shire" (and lives in it too, since the lion's shire is Ireland) constitutes an essential part of Mark–Earwicker's guilt.

The commercial, Roman nature of Mark should also remind us of the Rome–Amor anagram to which Campbell and Robinson call our attention (*Key*, 299). They interpret this dichotomy as applicable to the imperialism of Shaun and the "Christian love" of Shem. Mark is certainly Rome, not Amor. He leans toward Shaun's camp. In effect he sides with the acceptable, the practical, and must destroy or be destroyed by the rebellious values of selfless and unthinking love, epitomized by Tristan and Isolde.

Mark is one of the monolithic figures in *Finnegans Wake* in more ways than one. He is "a kingly man, of royal mien" (68:22), and one of the "lyonized mails" (465:15) of history; yet a statue or "manument" set up in his honor is shown little respect. For Mark is simply a conservative champion of the *status quo:* one of "the statues of our kuo" (58:19), he represents the "statuesquo" (181:34). Like the book in which he appears, he is a "onestone parable" (100:26 f.) of the rest of world, a monolith or "Monomark" (17:1). The "Monomark" reveals itself not as an honorable and dignified shaft, stele, or obelisk (68:29) but as a "mannikin pis," the sort of statue that charms with a Joycean mixture of lasting monumentality and absurd joke. The "Minnikin passe" undergoes several permutations: "Mannequins Pose" (267:n. 2), and "Mannequins pause! Longtong's breach is fallen down but Graunya's spreed's abroad" (58:11).

This latter pithy aphorism contains several intertwined themes. (1) London bridge is fallen down.

(2) Mark's clumsiness results in the loss of Graunya (which approximates the pronunciation of Grainne, the Isolde in the Irish version of the Tristan story). (3) "Longtong" resembles both the Russian general who relieves himself on the battlefield before Buckley's eyes and (4) Finnegan himself: "Grampupus is fallen down but grinny sprids the boord" (7:8 f.)—the board being the funeral meal of Finnegan's wake. Aside from the masculine symbol lurking in "Longtong," we remember that (5) the policeman in *Finnegans Wake* is named Long Lally Tomkins, an echo of sheriff Long John Fanning in *Ulysses*. It is Mark's police-nature, his authority, that seems to render him objectionable. Later we see Mark associated with the police again, and perhaps with Long Lally in particular, in "langwedge" (73:1), "longfoot" (222:31), "longstone" (539:3), and so forth. And (6) perhaps it is not too farfetched to see the exile nature of Mark–Earwicker in "Longtong" as well, for in the genre of Irish tale to which the story of Diarmid and Grainne belongs, one of the standard episodes, the exile, is labeled "Longes."

As Mark is a teashop lion, so is he a king and god who suffers much the same sort of humiliation as does Earwicker. Mark is a capsule counterpart of HCE: "Mark as capsules" (403:6). Mark shares the crime and fall of HCE. The embarrassment in the park with the girls and the soldiers is attributed to him as well as to HCE:

> — *Marak! Marak! Marak!*
> *He drapped has draraks an Mansianhase parak*
> *And he had ta barraw tha watarcrass shartcloths*
> *aff the arkbashap af Yarak!* [491:17–20]

Here the totem qualities of Mark are indicated by the meek rabbit (German: *Hase*) and the monkey (German: *Affe*), rendering the fall from monarchial lion more striking. The animal references are continued in "yarak," a term in falconry meaning *strength* or *ability,* usually applied to hawks.

Mark's personal misfortunes not only mirror those of

HCE; they are also intimately related to the health of his country. All of Ireland is a "land of lions' odor" (477:34); the country reflects the corruption and fall of its leader. In this sense Mark resembles Adam and Parnell as well as HCE when he falls "envenomoloped in piggotry" (99:19). The venom suggests the serpent in the Garden of Eden, while bigotry with a *p* suggests not only *pig*, but Piggot as well, the false accuser of Parnell. The fall of Adam and Parnell, also brought about primarily through the agency of a wife or mistress, is a parable or cause of a more general failure. Many share the suffering of the one. Mark too shares some of his peculiar failings with his country as a whole; his unwillingness to act, his age, and his infertility are also those of his impotent country, a mere shadow of what was or might be. Ultimately his failings are reverberations of the first, original, sin, which in *Finnegans Wake* is the sin of God Himself.

Mark, then, like HCE, runs the gamut of positions from the lowest to the highest. We meet him, like HCE, in several ruling positions. He appears as the lawgiver "King Jark" (558:17) and as "Shanator Lyons (475: 24 f.), in both cases with the similarity to public-spirited Jaun, or Shaun, built into his name. Mark ascends to supermundane positions as a "patriarchal shamanah" (75:14). When we meet him in the quartet, "madhugh, mardyk, luusk, and cong" (325:32), he has become Marduk, chief of the Babylonian deities. We know there is nothing strange about the combination of king and shaman, ruler and priest, in the same person —there are signs all through *Finnegans Wake* that Joyce knew Frazer's *Golden Bough*. But Mark falls to the very bottom too, down to the very mud as "mard" (374:1). There are indications that Mark is not to rule for long, that his corruption will call forth a new ruler, who, as a new version of the old ruler, will fall in his turn: "Leos, the next beast king. . . . I can feel you being corrupted" (466:6 f.). In the language of *Finne-*

gans Wake, fresh equals stale even before it appears. Whatever power is to replace power, it too is destined for corruption.

Finally, Mark is a mere shadow of his progenitor Finn, his prototype in the Irish Tristan and Isolde story, "that lionroar in the air . . . of Felin make Call" (488:13 f.). Unlike the heroic hunter Finn MacCool, Mark appears as a civilized and domesticated "Markwalther" (519:24), a forester (Walter means *man of the woods*), and, to bring his functions up to date, as "Corth examiner" into problems of plant fertility. Less roaring, less feline than Finn MacCool, Mark is a more modern and dispassionate dupe. In contrast to Finn, creator and hero of legend, Mark, both as king and as disciple, is merely a guardian or "custos" (532:1), the relic of a fabled greatness. He appears to be another of the many figures in *Finnegans Wake* who turn on the great wheel between god and beast; corrupted by virtue of its very success, authority is mocked by the rebels and usurpers who upset the old order to begin the cycle once more.

Joyce's birthplace, 41 Brighton Square West

The Liffey

By Dublin quays

6

The King in Finnegans Wake

THE NAMES and attributes of terrestrial dignitaries are punned into ridicule in *Finnegans Wake*. Although we find great men by the bushel, they almost always appear in demeaning disguise. We meet Abraham as "abramanation" (26:19 f.) or as "Allbrewham" (97:16), Sophocles as "Suffoclose" (47:19), Rameses as "ramescheckles" (452:21), and Henry II as the Mookse. Most of these kings and leaders seem to be varying incarnations of HCE himself, who appears as "William the Conk" (31:14), "Belly the First" (26:28), "woollem the farsed" (138:32), "Enwreak us wrecks" (545:23), and so forth. "Here Comes Everybody" is one of his most appropriate names.

Everyman–Earwicker usually rules or leads others; or example, as Noah, King Leary, Caesar, King Mark, Napoleon, or a Russian general. But he also falls prey to his successors, as the father gives way to his sons. In that cyclically organized world in which he sheds identities as deftly as a quick-change artist sheds costumes, he looks like the leading representative of his social order at one moment, but like its victim the next. By alternation or even simultaneously, he plays the roles of both priest and scapegoat. Not only does HCE often fall from recurring eminence; he is also reborn or recast. His story is an orgy of baptismal celebrations as much as it is a work of last rites.

HCE occupies a very "highpowered station" (557:30); his name is "Tyrannous" (71:17) and "King" (86:7). In one paragraph alone (611–612) as King Laegaire (pronounced *Leary*), he is called "High Thats Hight Uberking Leary," that is, the over-king; "Exuber High Ober King Leary very dead," including both German *über* and *ober;* "Most Highest Ardreetsar King," the "ard-righ" (pronounced *Ardree*) of Ireland being the king of Tara, or over-king, combined in "Ardreetsar" with the Russian Czar; "High High Siresultan Emperor"; "kirikirikiring"; "Highup Big Cockywocky Sublissimime Autocrat"; and "Hump cumps Ebblybally!" In this last expression we find a number of meanings compressed: (1) "Here comes everybody," (2) HCE's hump, (3) the Eblis, or Mohammedan evil spirit, (4) Eblana, or ancient Ireland, (5) the boll weevil, a bug similar to the earwig, which is at the foundation of the name Earwicker, (6) hemp, a "decoction" of which used to be dropped into the ear against earwigs, and (7) "Baile" or *ford,* part of the ancient and now revived Irish name for Dublin—the "town of the hurdle ford"—Baile-atha-cliath, pronounced *Blaclee.* Every part of the Irish hierarchy, from king and governor general on down, is somehow occupied by this one man; "the king, the Kovnor-Journal and *e*irenarch's *c*ustos *h*imself" ([531:36 f.]; italics mine).

The distortions by which HCE is made this king or that are usually varied and significant. For example: we discover that HCE himself, among other identities, is the reincarnated figure of the famous French hero and king, Vercingetorix (88:22), who suffered defeat at Caesar's hands. And from this identification proliferate a number of more or less recognizable variations tailored according to context: "Farseeingetherich" (54:3 f.), "Fierceendgiddyex" (66:12), "Valsinggiddyrex" (281: n. 1), "versingrhetorish" (346:19), and "Force in giddersh!" (617:12). Another warrior king, King Nebuchadnezzar, occurs as "Nobucketnozzler" (24:35) and

74

"Nobookisonester" (177:14); perhaps he is also related to the "Wulverulverlord" (74:4); for Nebuchadnezzar's illness late in life represents the classic case of lycanthropy, the insanity in which a man is said to bay at the moon and eat grass, imagining himself to have turned into a wolf. One of HCE's names too is *"Lycanthrope"* (71:32). Perhaps Joyce felt this disease an appropriate punishment for a ruler whose lust for power culminated in the destruction of Jerusalem. Wolves appear at least sixty times in *Finnegans Wake;* thus Joyce's references to wolves may have further as yet unexplored ramifications. Whatever they may turn out to be, we know that wolfish behavior, like almost any other overt display of physical brutality, was particularly unappealing to Joyce.

It is as autocrat and king, then, that HCE often falls, and fall he does. He is told to "Abedicate yourself." (379:19) and becomes a "Mocked Majesty" (380:4 f.). He is not only the "ardree," or high king, of Ireland, but also the poor pensioned-off soldier who accepts another "ardree's shilling" (49:4) for his services in the Crimean war. When, as pubkeeper, he has emptied the cups of his customers and falls drunk to the floor of the tavern, "he just slumped to throne" (382:26). That is, he falls as a king as well as hod-carrier Finnegan or publican Earwicker. His initials appear in the cry of his deposers: "Ho, croak, evildoer!" (532:3 f.), and in the judgment to which he is subjected: "haunted, condemned and execrated" (544:10 f.).

These attacks on kingship in *Finnegans Wake* are too comprehensive and varied to have been directed at but a single man. Other kings and the very position of king share the brunt of the assault. It would seem that, just as many of the insults borne by kings and other authorities in *Finnegans Wake* are also applicable to HCE, statements made about him are also judgments or opinions about other authorities found in the book.

Perhaps part of the reason for the unpleasant qualities of the kings mentioned in *Finnegans Wake* is that they are mostly English kings, kings who subjected Ireland to almost a millennium of victimization. The English redcoats who represented England to the Irish are apostrophized as a part of perifidious Albion, or England: "Porphyrious Olbion, redcoatliar" (264: n. 3). Joyce does not only have in mind "all the nuisances committed by soldats" (520:18), especially those of a foreign occupation: soldiers in general, and in particular those three soldiers who witness HCE's indiscretion in the park, represent the perfidious, libeling Albion, Blake's personification of England as a colonial and mercantile power. England, conqueror and lender, is "Englend" (170:32). Its exactions and cruelties call for a retaliatory revolution: "Every tub here spucks his own fat" (378:26 f.). That is, the tyrant-soldier Butt (*tub* reversed) calls forth or exudes (German: *spucken*) the counterforce of Taff (*fat*).

Thus a glossary of the English treatment of Ireland is not unreasonably a recounting of "the king's evils" (616:29), such as repression, dishonesty, incompetence. Richard III's appearances in *Finnegans Wake* are a case in point. He appears with his hump, one of his similarities to HCE, as "Crookback" (134:11) or as "Dook Hookbackcrook" (127:17), an indication of his by-hook-or-by-crook methods. His "a horse! a horse!" appears as "My fault, his fault, a kingship through a fault!" (193:31 f.). Here the principle and the example of it are cited simultaneously: kingship is obtained by a fault (usurpation? crime?) and this confession is made by the very king who can serve as a classic example of criminal brutality and tyranny: Shakespeare's "writchad the thord" (138:33) himself.

A correlative expression emerges later, in the more confused context of the tavern brawl during which HCE's crimes are laid bare: "Heigh hohse, heigh hohse, our kingdom from an orse!" (373:15 f.). This cry encapsulates a message of several parts. Both (1) the working song from "Snow White" and (2) the desperate exclamation of Richard III are echoed. The chief purport of the statement is that (3) the Irish are descendants of the Norse invaders of Ireland and that (4) the ancestors spoke the Erse (Irish) language. This interpretation is supported by (5) the "kin" substitution in "kingdom" and by (6) the German *Hose* (trousers) hidden in the "horse"—trousers being an article of dress with sexual connotations in *Finnegans Wake*. (This pun on "Hosen" was a trick that had already appeared, in simpler form, in Molly Bloom's "met him pike hoses" in *Ulysses*.) Further, (7) trousers serve to hide the part of the body thinly disguised in "orse," which is also (8) the part apparently revealed by HCE in Phoenix Park, a revelation constituting the fall that leads to a new "kingdom," that is, a land of HCE's kin or *Kinder*. So we have here another of the many statements in *Finnegans Wake* that involve the decline or death of one order at the same time that a new "kingdom" is created to reign in its turn.

The egotism of Richard's lust for power is also noted in his name, "Reacher the Thaurd" (319:20); and we see it in his willingness to give up his kingdom again for a weapon with which to defend himself: "my oreland for a rolvever" (352:9). "Oreland" suggests that Ireland is a king's source of riches (ore), readily sacrificed for personal ends. Ore is involved when this same accusation is leveled at HCE: "his personal low outhired his taratoryism, the orenore under the selfhide" (359:2 f.). That is, a particular, personal urge to personal advancement underlies the political principle of territorialism, or national aggrandizement.

Many of the cuts at authoritarian figures in *Finnegans Wake* are directed at positions other than that of king. A senator, for instance, is called "Shunadure" (475:27 f.). Even such a simple title as "Herr" is rarely allowed to stand unaltered. "My herrings!" (538:18) is the form of address into which "Meine Herren" is turned.

"Hersirrs" (355:28) emerges from "Herrscher" (German: *ruler*). Another version of "Mein Herr" appears when HCE is imprisoned: "my dodear [shades of Dodgson] devere revered mainhirr was confined to guardroom" (492:16 f.). The "her" sound in "mainhirr" indicates the feminization or emasculation of the authority in question (this is a process applied to many characters in *Finnegans Wake*).

The "hir" spelling in "mainhirr" also indicates that a *menhir,* or monolithic monument, is meant. The form stands out more clearly in "manhere" (539:3 f.) or in one of Earwicker's fuller titles: "Maynhir Mayour, our boorgomaister" (568:16 f.). The authority here, that of a mayor or burgomaster, is not only seen as boorish but is perhaps also made to share some of the aggressive qualities of Richard de Burgo, thirteenth-century conqueror of Connacht, who established the Joyce clan in the mountains between Galway and Mayo. In addition, May (in "Mayour"), the common month of fertility rituals, and the "mais" (German: *corn* or *maize*) are found in connection with a menhir, a stone that may stand alone, but which also may be a part of a cromlech or ceremonial circle of stones, or part of a dolmen, a tomb. "Meynhir Mayour," then, associates the mayor with the appurtenances of some ancient ritual.

HCE is repeatedly associated with such components of religious rites, an association thoroughly worked into the fabric of the rises and falls of priests and kings in *Finnegans Wake*. As we shall see, these rises and falls are not purely chance. They are part of an inevitable ritual determined by a natural and universal order of growth and decay. The tapestry of history which we know *Finnegans Wake* to be depicts scores of such glory-and-downfall cycles—an enormously crowded and merry wheel-of-fortune in which we find more the ironic pathos of the epic than the tragedy of history. Seen at a distance, every fall is somehow a "happy fall"—the "Felix culpa" judgment of St. Augustine is woven everywhere through the dreamland of *Finnegans Wake*. For every idol that falls, another is raised up. The stronger an authority is, the harder it crashes; but another authority inevitably takes its place.

A great number of expressions in *Finnegans Wake* make it clear that the deposition of a leader is often a desirable event. Or, more generally put: leaders, per se, call for deposition. The hanging of a king is a satisfying phenomenon: "Hungkung! Me anger's suaged!" (457:7). Other means of doing away with kings are suggested. For instance: "Teak off that wise head!" (607:3); "hun men wend to raze a leader" (278:21), in which "raise" is probably suggested along with its exact contrary, "raze"; and "Tyrants, regicide is too good for you!" (162:1).

"This passing of order and order's coming" (277:19 f.) is repeatedly suggested in various contexts: some of them make clear that the deposition of authority is called for simply because new authorities are ripe for taking over:

> On his pinksir's postern, the boys had it, at Whit-weekend had been nailed an inkedup name and title, inscribed in the national cursives, accelerated, regressive, filiform, turreted and envenomoloped in piggotry: Move up. Mumpty! Mike room for Rumpty! By order, Nickekellous Plugg.

[99:16–21]

This order demands the placing of a new Humpty Dumpty on his wall: Earwicker must move off, just as he himself had replaced the fallen hod-carrier Finnegan. The brother-pair Mick and Nick lurks in "Mike" and "Nickekellous." The passage also suggests that St. Nick himself provides the impetus for a change by an order nailed up on a door, just as Luther's challenge was first displayed. The new order is appropriately proclaimed on the weekend of Whitsunday, when the descent of the Holy Spirit on Pentecost is celebrated. The message is written in the cursive style, that is, the style of connected letters, as in the famous Book of Kells. The message itself is described in this passage in parody of the Sir Edward Sullivan description of the Book of Kells. The order, which shows the enveloping venom of the forger Richard Piggot, demands a change of regime. The old mum or Humpty Dumpty is Earwicker, who, like Mohammed, is "humpty" because of the hump to his back—his followers sing "Humpty Dumpty Sat on a Wall" to him: *"Hombly, Dombly Sod We Awhile"* (415:14 f.). The one who wants to bring HCE to this "humple pesition" (390:32) is Nick, that is, HCE's son Shaun. Why Nick Plug? A plug, we remember, is not only a stopper for a hole, but also the bullet of an assassin. The bullet in everywhere in *Finnegans Wake* on its way; it is the shot that a certain Buckley repeatedly delivers at the Russian General, another cognomen of HCE. The whole of *Finnegans Wake* is a fusillade directed at the old powers, a fusillade in art form: a "ballet of Gasty Power" (346:20).

The new man, Rumpty, who is to take the old man's place, seems to share more than one of his father's traits: the "rump" in his name echoes the part of the body which the Russian General revealed to Buckley and HCE revealed to the two girls and the three soldiers— the revelation constituting the crime in the park. And the rump is the pink postern to which the message is attached. The *rum* in "Rumpty" also indicates HCE's position—that of a rum-selling tavern-keeper. Later in the chapter the "Hungkung" and "Humpty Dumpty" themes coalesce into another cognomen for HCE: "Hung Chung Egglyfella" (374:34).

The change in power indicated here is typical of the recurring revolutions, in biological as well as political arrangements, that the Viconian cycles of *Finnegans Wake* include—revolutions in the sense either of turning over or of throwing over. Rarely does the usurper seem much different from the incumbent. "Only is order othered. Nought is nulled. *Fuitfiat!*" (613:13 f.). As it was, so shall it be. Although Cain kills Abel, the two are, after all, nevertheless brothers. We have seen that "Mumpty" merely gives way to "Rumpty." Or the change is even less noticeable: *"Move up, Mackinerny! Make room for Muckinurney!"* (264:margin); or "Quake up, dim dusky, wook doom for husky!" (593:14 f.).

Joyce calls on the frames of both the Viconian theory of historical cycles and of the medieval wheel-of-fortune concept to encompass these periodic revolutions. And *Finnegans Wake* may also be regarded as a modern version of the medieval "Falls of Great Men." The evanescence of power is emphasized by any of these frameworks. "Guestermed with the nobelities, to die bronxitic in achershous!" (536:12 f.). He who was yesterday German: *gestern*) a guest of the nobility is today in the house of Acheron. But in addition Joyce shows his awareness of the rites of assassination discussed by Frazer in *The Golden Bough*. We have already noted that HCE is a "Mocked Majesty." This is to say that he is made fun of, but also that he is a pretense of a king, the kind of king set up for the purposes of a ceremony, only to be deposed again. This sense of the mimicry of true kingship was also latent in the *mime* ending of the "Sublissimime" title already quoted. It is obvious in HCE's title "Tykingfest" or "Festy King." He is a king for the purposes of a fest, a celebration—implicit in his position is his deposition. The figure that Jaun is going to meet in the following passage, for instance, is clearly a temporary king, not an "everynight king":

> The Vico road goes round and round to meet where terms begin. Still onappealed to by the cycles and unappalled by the recoursers. . . . 'tis a grand thing (superb!) to be going to meet a king, not an everynight king, nenni, by gannies, but the over-king of Hither-on-Thither Erin himself, pardee, I'm saying. [452:21–28]

Does the "nenni" in this passage refer to the priest-king of Aricia whose rites Frazer discussed—the priest of

Nemi? In the following passage the bellbearing St. Patrick seems to be giving the deathblow to the last of such rites, if "aspenking" refers to such a priest under the old druidism which Patrick replaced:

> So perhaps, agglaggagglomeratively asaspenking, after all and arklast fore arklyst on his last public misappearance, circling the square, for the death-fête of Saint Ignaceous Poisonivy, of the Fickle Crowd (hopon the sexth day of Hogsober, killim our king, layum low!) and brandishing his bell-bearing stylo, the shining keyman of the wilds of change. [186:10–16]

In effect the stylus or pen of the saint (and of Shem the Penman and Joyce, in the context) acts as the key to change, interrupting the old cycle to begin another, somewhat different cycle in its turn.[1]

Evidence comes to light during Earwicker's trial which shows that the central action of the book, the affair in the park involving Earwicker with the two girls and the three soldiers, represents not only the fall of man from grace, Humpty from his wall, and so forth, but also the fall of a priest-king in a wooded glade as a result of an armed ambush planned to usurp his place:

> But it oozed out in Deadman's Dark Scenery Court through crossexanimation of the casehardened testis that when and where that knife of knifes the treepartied ambush was laid (roughly spouting around half hours 'twixt dusk in dawn, by Water-hose's Meddle Europeic Time, near Stop and Think, high chief evervirens and only abfalltree in auld the land). [87:33–88:2]

The "treeparty" or druidical rite includes the three parties in Phoenix Park; that is, it is a tripartite ambush. It involves the "Sunday King" (276:27 f.)—"the old buzzerd" in Joyce's footnote—his queen, and a soldier. In this passage the paradox that the same man is both priest and blood sacrifice is dramatized in the contrast between the evergreen "high chief evervirens" (HCE's initials) and the "abfalltree"—the latter a tripartite pun encompassing garbage (German: *Abfall*), the fall from Eden, and the tree from which Eve plucked the apple (German: *Apfel*). The victor is also victim, as Joyce's conifer is also deciduous. That only three parties are involved is not unreasonable, since the two girls are often fused into one unit and the soldiers into another. Adaline Glasheen has pointed out that the two Issys are probably two halves of a split personality.[2] A few lines later this pair is again associated with HCE's ouster:

> Two dreamyums in one dromium? Yes and no error. And both as like as a duel of lentils? Peacisely. So he was pelted out of the coram populo, was he? Be the powers that be he was. The prince in principel should not expose his person? Macchevuole!
>
> [89:3–7]

That is, the two "yummy" twins of the dream are like one Dromio—the twins in Shakespeare's *Comedy of Errors*. HCE is belted out of the heart of the people, the "Fickle Crowd," by violating Machiavelli's precept that a ruler must not expose himself to danger unnecessarily. ("Macchevuole" says "do as you like"—German: *mache*, Italian: *vuole*.) But HCE has "exposed" himself to the other parties of the "treepartied ambush." He has passed his own "stonehinged gate" (69:15)—we note the suggestion of Stonehenge—thus "tempting gracious providence by a stroll on the peoplade's eggday, unused as he was yet to being freely clodded" (69:28 f.). The twins-ouster association, incidentally, always involves food (in the passages just cited, apples and lentils and eggs) and suggests that the victim is finally eaten: "twinsome bibs but hansome ates, like shakespill and eggs!" (161:30 f.). Like his son Shem, HCE is "CelebrAted!" (421.21) in the grim trencher of Ate, goddess of vengeance.

There are other indications that the fallen king is a King of the Wood. He is addressed as "noble fir" (100:14) rather than "sir," has a "sylvan family tree"

(522:17), is danced around as a "seedfather" (55:8), a "gigantig's lifetree" (55:27), and so forth. He is dismembered "with discrimination for his maypole" (358:34), and his murder is completed under the green boughs of his tree:

As hollyday in his house so was he priest and king to that: ulvy came, envy saw, ivy conquered. Lou! Lou! They have waved his green boughs o'er him as they have torn him limb from lamb.   [58:5 ff.]

The progression from old king to new, and the subsequent rejection of the new king become old, is effectively summed up in such a passage as this:

The keyn has passed. Lung lift the keying!
— God save you king! Muster of the Hidden Life!
— God serf yous kingly, adipose rex!

[499:13–16]

The king has passed, says the first voice. The old king is a murderer, a Cain. Our lungs lift up the new king: long live the king. The new king is commended as master, muster, and prototype of more exalted realms (*Muster:* German for *pattern* or *prototype*); he is a divine representative. The next line is one of those typically self-contradictory Joycean sentences, turning "God serve you kindly, Oedipus Rex!" into something like "May God enslave you royally, overweight king!" The new king, in other words, is hailed as successor to the old, but within two lines his fall in invoked and he is made ridiculous. This inevitable turn of events is also indicated in the title of the pantomime summing up the history of Earwicker and his family: *"Oropos Roxy and Pantharhea"* (513:21 f.). According to J. S. Atherton's exhaustive analysis of this title,[3] "Oropos Roxy" represents Earwicker as well as Oedipus Rex, since "Oropos is "soporo" (I sleep) written backward, and the rock or sleeping giant is one of Earwicker's signatures in *Finnegans Wake*. "Pantharhea" fits in several ways: primarily in representing the doctrine of Heraclitus, "panta rhei" (everything flows), but also because it seems to include the panther mentioned later; the "phanthares" (565:19); Panthera, the "spousebreach" Roman soldier mentioned in *Ulysses*, supposedly the father of Jesus Christ; Rhea, who gave Saturn rocks to eat; and Rhea, the mother of the twins Romulus and Remus, founders of Rome and surrogates for the sons of Earwicker: Shem and Shaun.

The identification of HCE with Oedipus Rex suggests the similarities between them: concern with the succession of power, parent-child difficulties, incest, the generation of two children who are deadly enemies, the speedy development from rise to fall, and so forth. HCE himself is said to have an "eatupus complex" (128:36). In addition, what we think of as the myth of Oedipus embodies, perhaps consciously, the additional and probably older myth that postulates an intimate connection between the health and well-being of a ruler and the fertility and prosperity of his country: the patricide and incest of Oedipus were said to result in the pestilence that afflicted his people. This belief in the effect of a ruler's personal situation on the health of his country was as firmly held in ancient Ireland as elsewhere.[4] Joyce suggests this belief in *Finnegans Wake*. But another belief about kings receives an even more insistent emphasis in the book: power itself is a corrupting influence. Inevitably the king slips in virtue; inevitably the usurper stands ready, as yet uncorrupted, to take his place and reign until he, in turn, suffers the inevitable fall.

7

The Wake *Pantheon*

WE HAVE SEEN that Joyce's exploration of the modalities
of the possible in *Finnegans Wake* does not dissolve
into a rampant anarchism: neither in matter nor in technique. The disintegration of his language repeats the
Osiris myth in verbal form, and the dismemberment is
followed by a methodical reconstitution. In other words,
not quite all the modalities of the possible are really
explored. God's names and attributes are distorted in
multitudinous ways so as to denigrate the honor of God,
but rarely to glorify it.

Joyce is, in fact, careful in his treatment of his various
heroes and gods, not simply because what is conventionally exalted can be readily distorted downward,
whereas the transfiguration of the exalted into something yet higher is difficult. The Buddha, for instance,
whose name would seem to be a ready target for all sorts
of schoolboyish jests, simply appears as "buddhy"
(234:14) or "buddhoch" (25:25); *hoch* (German:
high) is merely appended to his name. He never sinks
any lower than "Sid Arthar" (59:7) and "Sirdarthar"
(347:9), innocuous Arthurian variations on his name
Siddhartha. Bruno of Nola, Swift, and Sterne, each of
whom appears scores of times in the course of the book,
are not badly treated. Jesus Christ receives the utmost
respect, as does the Virgin Mary. But generals, kings,
and popes—men of power and influence—come off less

86

well. And little glory is attached to any of the patriarchal figures who act as surrogates for the central figure HCE, gods and God among them. It is on a par with these attitudes that God as a prescriptive and authoritarian concept is treated with a most varied and ingenious harshness. By virtue of a species of divine right the divinities that flit in and out of the pages of this book have abuse and contumely heaped upon them.

Admittedly, on rare occasions Joyce allows a god to be called "good." But this slight admixture of the favorable with the negative is consonant with Joyce's pervasive principle of modification and qualification; the final definition of any phenomenon is always checked and hedged against. God cannot be simply the butt of unrelieved insult. A first essential of Joyce's neologisms and puns is the inclusion in a statement of its own refutation. For example: "My heeders will recoil with a great leisure . . ." (160:35). Joyce enjoys the confrontation of opposites within a single term: "any way words all in one soluble." This principle of inconsistency which Joyce held to in sculpturing his language also operates in his simultaneous obeisance to and thumbing of the nose at the gods. Joyce seems to have meant his theology as well as his poetry to demonstrate Bruno of Nola's doctrine of the identity of opposites.

We should note that the *Finnegans Wake* god is only in part and at times the Christian deity. For one thing, Joyce's god is Everygod, as Earwicker is Everyman and his antagonists are "everyknight" (126:18). This alone makes it difficult to identify Joyce's gods. For another, we shall see that the gods in the book are often remarkably similar to Humphrey Chimpden Earwicker. Joyce may not particularly care to make the dreams of his hero fit with what we might expect of a Chapelizod publican (who could hardly converse in a dozen languages about the arcane mysteries that two millennia of civilization have debated), yet much of the book does seem to reach us only after filtering through its hero's sensibilities, and the filter modifies what passes through it. In other words, the congruencies between various divinities and HCE may be explained by an intensely anthropomorphic view of the heavenly powers. If we see and must see our gods in terms of our own qualities, insofar as *Finnegans Wake* is HCE's narration the gods reflected in the book must bear the features of HCE. Their inadequacies reflect HCE's sense of guilt, and they have abuse flung at them in the dreamer's effort to punish himself for his crimes.

The main recipient of this abuse seems to be the Christian god. Just what Joyce has against him in particular appears in the distorted locutions in which his names and attributes are presented.

God as a Conservative Force

One of the complaints against God is that he is fossilized, out of date, like many of the high powers in the "allnights newseryreel." Although the creative force of God is not denied him anywhere in *Finnegans Wake*, his power, like that of other authoritarian figures, is not in ascendance.

This paradox between creativity and decline is everywhere apparent in *Finnegans Wake*. We see it, for instance, in the sentence "*Our lorkmakor he is proformly annuysed*" (342:28). The activity of the Lordmaker or Lord Mayor here is to lurk, as we see by comparing "lorkmakor" with the "lork" element in the line "Sherlook is lorking for him" (534:31). The "nuyse" or noise of God is the thunder in Viconian theory and consonant enough with our conventional assumptions about divine activity, at least if we ignore certain scurrilous hints from Joyce as to how God produces the noise. But "proformly" suggests the opposite of profundity, and the "ennui" in "annuysed" cancels whatever dignity may have been suggested by "profoundly annoyed."

There are other ways in *Finnegans Wake* in which the mere formality of God's present position is contrasted with God's originally creative function. God is frequently a fish; he is addressed as "Cod" (54:20), for instance. The fish image, an old fertility symbol, is clearly phallic, that is, creative, in *Finnegans Wake;* but "Cod" also suggests that God is a joke ("cod" equals "joke" in the schoolboy parlance of the *Portrait*). The latter sense of "cod" appears in one of Joyce's versions of the commandment "Thou shalt have no other Gods before me"—"No cods before Me" (579:21 f.). God also appears with appurtenances we associate with Leopold Bloom: "Caius Cocoa Codinhand" (467:13). The portrait is drawn like that of Chaucer's Priapus in "The Parliament of Fowls," symbolic weapon in hand. The references to God as a cod recur frequently. "God knows" is written as "Kod knows" (247:16); His staff of office is "codhead's mitre" (233:16); the German "Lobet Gott den Herrn" (Praise God and Lord) becomes "Loab at cod then herrin" (587:2), which in turn echoes a number of references to God as a herring. Another fish is identified with God when we read that the creation reveals "cods' cradle and porpoise plain" (427:20 f.). Many of Joyce's cod-references also show a consciousness of the article of clothing, the codpiece, the associations of which match the fertility symbol of the fish. Of course it is a symbol with pagan as well as Christian overtones. The Christian God is only one of a number of "fishygods" (4:1 f.) in the fluid element of *Finnegans Wake*.

Codes

Cod is not only fish; it also implies "code," the set of commandments which are the instruments of authority. The code is the authority that HCE puts to the test in his "Guilty but fellows culpows!" (363:20) confession. His crimes against propriety are called "The code's proof" (363:36 f.). The laws of the thundering fish-god, "A dondhering vesh vish, *Magnam Carpam*" (525:20), are "the propriety codestruces of Carprimustimus"

(108:12 f.). Joyce also turns the English translation of the Jesuit motto, "For the greater glory of God," into "for the greeter glossary of code" (324:21), suggesting the stabilizing, regulating function of religion, rather than its creative mission. (Two lines later the Latin abbreviation of the same motto, AMDG, is set forth as "Am. Dg." [324:23], seemingly a statement of the Lord Himself that He is a dog. We are reminded of the play in *Ulysses* with the God-dog dichotomy. As we shall see, God is turned into a number of other animals in *Finnegans Wake*.)

There is little doubt about what Joyce thinks of the "old's code" (14:21); it is always associated with the passing order, the world ripe for replacement. "We will not say it shall not be, this passing of order and order's coming (277:18 ff.). In *Finnegans Wake* codes and creeds smell of the brutality of the Ku Klux Klan: "the hidebound homelies of creed crux ethics" (525:1 f.); the word *cross,* implicit in the word "crux," suggests that Christianity's creed is not excluded from the epithet "hidebound." The hidebound homily of the catechism is elsewhere associated with the Ku Klux Klan: "K. K. Katakasm" (533:24). Similarly an alderman satisfied with the *status quo* is called "olderman K. K. Alwayswelly" (365:30). In an evil moment HCE himself becomes a "cruxader" and shows off to a "crowd of the Flu Flux Fans" (464:15). That part of the court to which the accused HCE thinks of turning is called "Determined Codde or Cucumber Upright" (536:33). Here again the fertilizing potency as well as the fossilized rigidity of the "old's code" is indicated. The code supports the *status quo;* it is a conservative influence. God speaks against change: "as it was let it be, says he!" (80:23).

Set in opposition or in answer to the old codes is another code which permeates *Finnegans Wake*. This code demands a continual, cyclical upheaval rather than the vindication of the *status quo*. Nature's will demands nothing less than the overthrow of the old order, as we see from the following passage: "for the farmer, his son and their homely codes, known as eggburst, eggblend, eggburial and hatch-as-hatch can" (614:31 ff.). Here the Father, the Son, and the Holy Ghost are identified with the three most important Viconian ages: birth, flourishing or marriage, the decline. Together with the "recorso," the evolution into the next cycle of man, the four-stage cycle is paralleled by the four books of *Finnegans Wake*. This "homely" code is the only one presented favorably in the work; it exacts the destruction of other codes.

When any other code does appear, Joyce almost inevitably associates it with the unpleasant, with an officer of the law, for instance, as in "sherif Toragh" (29:17). The law itself is the "lag" (603:25) or the "lax" (573:33) or the "low" (359:3) or a "lie" (223:28). The sneering at code and law is shot through with references to the censors who looked at Joyce's work "through their gangrene spentacles" (397:35) and decided to suppress it, to "regul their reves by incubation." Joyce's animus is directed at the Irish codes as well as at the English and is only partially tempered by a simultaneous attachment to the civil and religious institutions that remain such a substantial part of his subject matter. Like language, which shows its force and beauty best by being altered and opposed, the old codes still exert their fascination in the context of a "cyclological" book mirroring a "cyclological" world.

Doubts about the Church of Rome

Certainly the case for an overriding anti-authoritarianism, anti-God purpose in *Finnegans Wake* can be easily overstated. Much of the pseudotheological conflict in which the characters engage is presented dramatically, and not with any obvious intent to teach. Since the arguments are dramatically or artistically effective rather than didactically forceful, they are better viewed from

Joyce's aesthetic standpoint than from a theoretical one —a standpoint that is too likely to misuse *Finnegans Wake* as a "pièce à thèse." In the opposition between the English church and Rome, for instance, both the "dirtynine articles" (534:12) of the one church and the "plague" of the other are repeatedly presented: "No martyr where the preature is there's no plagues like rome" (465:34 f.). Undeniably the "Rome" of this motto occupies the position of the "home" in the saying that is parodied; Rome shares with the concept of home the onus of meddling authority as well as the value of a security-giving social institution.

Generally Joyce groups Rome with other objectionable authorities: "Our island, Rome and duty!" (374:19); the orthodox theology itself is a dragon of "baskatchairch theologies (there werenighn on thaurity herouns in that alraschil arthouducks draken)" (358:28 ff.). In addition to the name of Haroun al Raschid in this statement, we read that the orthodox and successful (Sanskrit: *artha*) rascal dragon (German: *Drachen*) has spawned nine theologies of authority; the thirty-nine articles of the Anglican Church and nigh on thirty heroines—the twenty-nine girls who will in turn kill and dismember the old God, "disassembling and taking him apart" (358:33).

The Patriarch

The authoritarian or patriarchal side of the church is presented inevitably with overtones of laughter or belittlement—always in some manner that states or implies rejection. St. Patrick himself appears as "Slypatrick" (51:8), "Mr Trickpat" (487:23), "Trichepatte" (228:6), "partnick" (478:26), or as "diupetriark" (153:27), in which he associated with God (dieu), the rock of Peter's church, the ark, and inevitably with the rank of patriarch. This rank is both his glory, and in Joyce's view, his limitation. Patrick's version of Peter's church makes him appear as "Paddrock" (611:2); he has "padded" the rock of Peter. Like Mark and the other great fathers, Patrick is also feminized, as "Madre Patriack" (408:32). And St. Patrick seems to nibble in the pantry of Ireland as "our pantriarch of Comestowntonobble" (74:11) and to reduce his host as he himself grows in glory. The patriarch in *Finnegans Wake* is a meddler, putting his "pastryart's noas" (531:11) where he shouldn't. The wonder is that on a rare occasion he can still be "sympatrico" (464:16).

Like any other authority, the power of the patriarch is to be more regretted as it grows. In the maxim "the greater the patrarc the griefer the pinch" (269:24 f.), Lord Acton's theory that power corrupts finds its clearest exposition. In "the main the mightier the stricker the strait" (512:14 f.) we encounter the same idea: an increase of power provides the means to an increase of oppression. It is power, not right, that wins the battle: "To the vast go the game!" (512:15). A cognate maxim appears later in reference to Persse O'Reilly, or Perce Oreille, one of the Earwicker substitutes: "The whacker his word the weaker our ears for auracles who parles parses orileys" (467:28 f.). These few words are not very mellifluous, but they contain a good deal of meat. "Auracles" refers to ears as well as to "oracles," while "parses orileys" includes not only Perce Oreille (French for *earwig*) or Persse O'Reilly (Earwicker) but one of the many references to language teaching in *Finnegans Wake:* parsing orally. The strength of "whacker" is augmented by the sense of *brave* or *zealous* (German: *wacker*). It is this German spelling we find later in "Lugh the Brathwacker will be listened after" (594:19 f.), which refers to Lugh of the Long Arms, the Irish hero of whom Cuchulinn was the reincarnation. In other words, Lugh (or Cuchulinn) compels attention by means of superior strength. "The whacker his word" apparently refers to writers generally and to Joyce in particular, who shares the guilt of violence in that he forces a hearing by giving his language unusual wrenches. The self-accusation sounds like a rueful echo of "the greater the patrarc the griefer the pinch." Whether patriarch or poet, St. Patrick or Petrarc, he who applies force seems to arouse that much more antagonistic resistance.

Other Clerics

Joyce infuses many references to churchly positions with the double concept of toadying to those above and oppressing those below. The rites of the ecclesiastical rock are "bevelled" by functionaries who are themselves a little too aggressive: "Bisships, bevel to rock's rite!" (606:13). This is also an injunction to bishops to simplify their practices to approximate the rites of Peter's church. Since "biss" is German for bite, the distortion of "bishop" introduces a suggestion of viciousness. The same German word appears in the coinage "Bissavolo" (68: 19). The Italian "bisavolo," or "great father," is a respectful term applied to patriarchal figures, a term with which Dante refers to Caccia Guida. As is standard in *Finnegans Wake*, the term of respect is turned in the direction of insult. We shall see below how God Himself is invested with very aggressive appetites, for food as well as for sexual gratification, both of which may be suggested in "Bisships." That the bite in "Bisships" is not primarily for gastronomic purposes is suggested by an earlier passage: "Ambras! Ruffle her! Bussing was before the blood and bissing will behind the curtain. Triss!" (467:5 ff.). The embrace suggested in this passage is the embrace of St. Patrick and Ireland, also the embrace of Tristan and Isolde. The inflammatory style of the exhortation is that in which the whole sermon of Jaun (Shaun) is couched. It is interesting that much of what Jaun says is put in a hortative, commanding way. Like Buck Mulligan, Jaun tries to present his most objectionable expressions in a charming, positively engaging style.

In Jaun's sermon the clerical appetite is at its most

94

voracious. The biss-bite-hips combination of "Bisships" figures again in the food-sex advice he throws to his charges: "And, by the bun, is it you goes bisbuiting His Esaus and Cos and then throws them bag in the box? . . . Hip confiners help compunction. Never park your brief stays in the men's convenience" (433:20–25). Of course "His Esaus and Cos" reveals by its initials that HCE is meant, that the girls are in the process of eating him up. Shaun's most unorthodox sermon ends in a very food-conscious tirade of theological fragments: "I'll try my set on edges grapeling an aigrydoucks, grilled over birchenrods, with a few bloomancowls in albies" (456:15 f.). The vinegared ducks with cauliflower (German: *Blumenkohl*) into which Shaun intends to sink his teeth in this passage seem to be the orthodoxies (in "aigrydoucks") with which he is perpetually struggling.

In part the brother-fight in *Finnegans Wake* is set in terms of a struggle between schismatic elements of the Catholic church. In one of the first fights between Shem and Shaun the question is aired: which one is "art-thoudux" and which is "heterotropic" (252:20). We see that of the two brothers, Shaun is the success—*artha* is Sanskrit for *successful*. Shaun, the very type of an oppressive colonialist, missionary, and self-justifying exploiter, labels Joycelike Shem, the outsider, a "doctator" (170:22) or a "Digteter" (423:18). Again the food-reference in Shaun's speech, this time to potato digging. Shaun claims the highest orthodoxy for himself. One passage in which he heaps abuse on his rival and brother particularly deserves quotation. Shaun claims that he could write as effective a book as Shem, but that his book would convey only the most orthodox beliefs:

> I'd pinsel it with immenuensoes as easy as I'd perorate a chickerow of beans for the price of two maricles and my trifolium librotto, the authordux Book of Lief, would, if given to daylight, (I hold a most incredible faith about it) far exceed what that bogus bolshy of a shame, my soamheis

95

brother, Gaoy Fecks, is conversant with in audible
black and prink. Outragedy of poetscalds! Acom-
edy of letters!   [425:18–24]

The burden of this passage is that Shaun claims he could
paint (German: *Pinsel*) his book with innuendoes to
his amanuenses (as Mohammed dictated the Koran) as
easily as he could speak like Cicero to produce miracles;
that his tripartite libretto (echo of the tripartite life of
St. Patrick, the trinity, and the threefold source of information, the three soldiers who witnessed the crime
in the park), slightly broken (Italian: *rotto*), would
constitute the orthodox book of belief, far exceeding
the work of his hot (German: *heiss*) brother, who is a
counterfeit, Bolshevist shame (Shem), a Guy Fawkes.
That brother is not only Guy and gay, but also a goy
(Yiddish for *gentile* or *outsider*). Another passage, "For
hugh and guy and goy and jew" (273:13 f.), indicates
that Joyce probably had this additional sense in "Gaoy"
in mind.

Shaun's aggressive and political attacks on his enemy
do appear, in their context in *Finnegans Wake*, more
admirable than the sort of fawning and obsequious behavior religious duties often elicit—although Shaun
himself lapses into such obsequiousness too. The pray-
ing of the monk, for instance, is a natural butt of Joyce's
humor: "clerks have surssurhummed" (15:15). This expression occurs at the beginning of an ever-renewed
black-massing of the Catholic ritual. "Sir" is spelled
"sur" to fit with the *sursum corda* prayer ("Let us lift up
our hearts")—the cords of the *sursum corda* appearing
three lines below. Later the opening of the "Angelus,"
"Behold the handmaid of the Lord!" is coupled with the
sursum corda in the same profane manner in which
Shaun speaks to his flock, and in which Joyce speaks
about God: "Upsome cauda! Behose our handmades for
the lured!" (239:9 f.). The "cor," or heart, of the original *sursum corda* becomes a "cauda" or tail, and the
Lord is "lured"—certainly not a very orthodox sug-

gestion on Joyce's part, although it may fit the Greco-Roman notions of divine behavior and be called for by a full exploration of the implications implicit in God as the "Maker."

Like the authority and dignity of God, the authority and dignity of the divine service is degraded and ridiculed, as are the churchmen who "serve" this service to their congregations. The anthropomorphic suggestion that God may be lured is only one of many such suggestions in *Finnegans Wake*. In a moment we shall see how thoroughly God is called low and lewd in the course of the book—not only in parodies of the mass, but in the Lord's Prayer and other contexts as well.

God's Lowness

It is in the transformations of the name of God himself that Joyce exerts all his ingenuity. We have noted for comparison how gently the Buddha is treated. And Christ is not insulted either as is God the Father. Christ appears in such combinations as "muddy kissmans" (11:14), "joysis crisis" (395:32), and "christous pewmillieu" (552:28). In the latter, the milieu of pious Christians is where they mill about: as occupants of a pew. "Pewmillieu" also suggests Russian "pomeelooie" (Russian for *have mercy*). At worst Christ is "crush": "*for crush sake*" (271:margin). God the Father, on the other hand, is subjected to a gamut of opprobrious analyses, which, although they are mutually contradictory at many points, are fairly consistent in ridicule or condemnation.

Most commonly the Allhighest is invested with the lowest qualities. Part of the Joycean Lord's Prayer runs: "So may the low forget him their trespasses" (615:36); again Joyce plays on the idea of God's smallness by parodying Hamlet's statement of faith: "the diminitive that chafes our ends" (278:n. 2).

The lowness of God is also expressed in puns like "pease Pod" (412:31) for "please God," or worse: "the wrath of Bog" (76:31) and "O moy Bog" (416:19); the exclamation "Load Allmarshy!" (17:8) suggests this judgment of God as a bog, which also happens to be Russian for *god*. The idea occurs repeatedly (485:6, 560:14 f., 567:6).

In other locutions God turns animal. The Jesuit motto, AMDG, turns, as we have seen, into "Am. Dg." (324:23). God is also presented as dog in "Dogs' vespers are anending" (276:11), whereas in "offgott affsang" (346:22) we see a half-God, half ape (German: *Affe;* French: *singe*). In one exclamation, "laus sake" (27:8), we find the Latin for "praise" and the German spelling of "louse" in palimpsest below the negroid pronunciation of "lord." (Louse is also an appropriate epithet for Lucifer, as in the utterance about him and the Book of the Dead: "Since the lausafire has lost and the book of the depth is. Closed." [621:2 f.])

God as the "primum mobile" has a monolithic appearance, like HCE: "the top primomobilisk" (163: 21 f.). But He also appears as the bottom of the barrel, the lees, when the prime mover or "primum mobile" becomes "primeum nobilees" (356:11). To the decline of the Christian God Joyce applies the German term *Götterdämmerung*, the twilight of the gods:

> Boildoyle and rawhoney on me when I can beuraly forsstand a weird from sturk to finnic in such a patwhat as your rutterdamrotter. Onheard of and umscene! Gut aftermeal! See you doomed.
>
> [17:13–16]

This statement by Jute, the cad in the park, indicates that Joyce regards his book as a species of "rutterdamrotter," that is, Götterdämmerung. The gods in *Finnegans Wake* rest in twilight; they are never glorified. Jute's objection to the mixtures of Gaelic and Roman elements in the argument of his antagonist Mutt may also very well be Joyce's notion of how a hypothetical reader might react to the first dozen pages of his book.

98

Translated roughly, the passage reads: "Boiled oil and raw honey on me if I, a buttery-interested (French: *beurre*) Butt-like person, can barely reason out (German: *Verstand*) an English word (Irish *beurla*: the English language) from start to finish, from your Turkish to your Finnic tongues, in such a patois as that of your Rotterdam-rotting-rutting damn writer. Unheard of and obscene!" The language of *Finnegans Wake* does indeed seem to echo the sound of a thorough disintegration of the gods.

God's Lewdness

The polylingual mission of *Finnegans Wake,* expressed in "from sturk to finnic," is also expressed in another passage which ascribes a further sort of lowness to God: "Boumce! It is polisignstunter. The Sockerson boy. To pump the fire of the lewd into those soulths of bauchees" (370:30 f.). The fire of the Lord is cast as lust (we have noted this in "lured"), a notion enforced by the *bauch* or *baccio* in "bauchees": the first is German for stomach; the second, Italian for kiss. In one term, "Gotopoxy" (386:31), several of these concepts of the contamination of God's orthodoxy are compressed into one word. The "rut" in "rutterdamrotter" points in the same direction, the lewdness of God. Perhaps this is another quality that God shares with HCE. We note that one of HCE's names is "Rutter" (88:21, 593:6) as well, and that he is "the rudacist rotter in Roebuckdom" (90:26 f.). The creativity of fatherhood, whether of God or of man, seems inevitably to imply sexuality.

The idea of God's lust is explored in another way. Joyce links the trinitarian nature of the Creator with His sexual creative nature, if we recognize threefold quantities as symbolically sexual. Here is a passage presenting the union of Earwicker and Anna Livia in a mixture of Olympian and vulgar points of view:

The threelegged man and the tulippied dewydress.
Lludd hillmythey, we're brimming to hear!
[331:8 f.]

Here threeleggedness refers both to the creative trinity
and to sexuality. A "threelegged man" is also presuma-
bly a man who walks with a stick, like the old man in
the riddle of the sphinx. In other words, the male in
this passage, whether HCE or triune God, is old, whereas
the female, the river in her two-lipped pied-with-flow-
ers dress (the banks and the foliage floating on the
water) is repeatedly rejuvenated and renewed. The
notion of extreme age applied to HCE as well as to
God appears earlier on the same page: "He's herd of
hoarding and her faiths is altared" (331:3). A few lines
later the same idea is repeated once more: "So in the
names of the balder and of the sol and of the hollichrost, ogsowearit, trisexnone" (331:14 f.).

Here "balder" indicates the aging father as well as
Balder, son of Odin; the "sol" is the sun or son, Jesus
Christ. "Balder" must also refer to the cliffs of the hill
of Howth, as in "lludd hillmythey"—in Joycean myth
the male counterpart to Dublin's feminine element,
which is the river Liffey in her "tulippied dewydress."
"Ogsowearit" suggests the worn nature of the Irish
pagan heaven, Tir-nan-og, the land of youth. And in
"trisexnone" is expressed the three-in-one of the trinity,
as well as its creative growth (three sexes in one) in its
three-six-nine (-none) progression. Joyce explores the
same progression elsewhere, as in this "Old King Cole"
(Finn MacCool) variation: "Terce for a fiddler, sixt for
makmerriers, none for a Cole" (619:27 f.).

God as Goat

The tendency to lower God by investing Him with low
sexual drives is worked out in a highly elaborate treatment of God as goat. We have seen in a compound like
"Gotopoxy" (386:31) a fusion of the idea of orthodoxy
and contamination—in *got a pox* or *Gott a pox*. The

additional suggestion of goat is of particular interest. God's lewdness is emphasized not only in the ways we have seen but in this additional animalization as well. As the fish may be a religious symbol and a fertility symbol, a goat too is both a classically lecherous animal and the animal of the cult of Dionysius.

God is repeatedly called a goat and has the hairiness of the goat ascribed to him. We read: "So help her goat and kiss the bouc" (94:29), in which the "bouc" is the book, the mouth, or cheek, and the male goat or buck (French: *bouc*). "Please God" becomes "plays goat" (347:15), which is exactly what God does in *Finnegans Wake*. Often the goat occurs with other animals—sheep for instance: "they wonted to get out by the goatweigh afore the sheep was looset" (372:13); and "hiding that shepe in his goat" (373:13 f.), in which the hump shape under HCE's coat is meant. God is called a goat or given hircine qualities in one way or another at least forty times more. Some of these references show that Joyce had the Jacob and Esau story in mind, in which Jacob (Shem) defrauds Esau (Shaun) of Isaac's blessing by simulating the brother's hairiness with a goatskin. HCE is Isaac to his own two sons, and shares with one of them the divine and goatlike hairiness; he is "Erin's hircohaired culoteer" (275:1 f.) and "Hircups Emptybolly!" (321:15). The sheep-goat opposition that recurs in reference to HCE must reflect an old idea of the natural pairing of these opposites—an idea expressed in "tell the sheep from the goats" and in the traditional representation of the divine princes, Christ and Satan, as lamb and goat. The goat is somehow involved in the relationships of God and Isaac and HCE to the brother-pairs vying for their fathers' favor, but the parallels are not easy to define.

The goats in *Finnegans Wake* occur in conjunction with fish even more than with lamb. Fish are naturally associated with the impulse of life. Anna Livia is the "Brook of Life, backfrish!" (264:6 f.). She is the constantly renewed life-force of water, flowing into the ocean to return again fresh; "backfrish" is also a "Backfisch," a German term for a young fish suitable for frying and for an inexperienced adolescent girl—therefore the fresher part of the River Liffey. Anna Livia is not only fish, but goat too: "she ninnygoes nannygoes nancing by" (7:27) and identifies herself with a she-goat (Latin: *capra*) when she goes to some paternal goat, who may be her husband Bacchus, or her maker: "at long leash I'll stretch more capritious in his dapplepied bed." (276:n. 5). Like her male counterparts, the chief female deity of the book bears a number of animal identifications which help define her character as well as link her with her mythological prototypes.

The relation of goats to fish in *Finnegans Wake* apparently is based on their symbolic significance in the Dionysian, the Christian, and other religions. Each animal embodies a life-force; each animal suggests fertility and has its time-honored place in primitive religious worship. Joyce works on the basis of the fish-Christ association: "Pass the fish for Christ's sake!" (535:25). He equates the two one-syllabled animals with each other in a footnote:

> [3]Pure chingchong idiotism with any way words all in one soluble. Gee each owe tea eye smells fish. That's U.   [299:n. 3]

One would think that g-h-o-t-i spells goat, although a two-syllabled goat. But here goat and fish are identical. The immediate source of the word "ghoti" is G. B. Shaw, who showed that "fish" could be spelled "ghoti" if one took the "f" sound, written as "gh" as in "cough," added the "i" sound, written as "o" in "women," and finally the "sh" sound which the "ti" in a word like "caution" signals. Thus "ghoti" spells "fish." Perhaps the "eye" spelling is also a reference to a ewe, as "aye" is in the following: "Whenin aye was a kiddling. And the tarikies held sowansopper. Let there beam a frishfrey" (356:16 f.). We move again from goat (kid) to fish:

the fish are fresh fish fry, which is to accompany a sowing supper (a feast of fertility?), a supper announced in the style of God's creation in *Genesis:* "Let there be. . . ."

The "tarikies" in the previous quotation are apparently "darkies" (cannibals?) whose darkness is to be offset by the "beam" of eating fish. Perhaps fish-eating here refers to communion as well, or to the Christian habits of diet on Friday. But it may also be that fish-eating is God-eating (we have noted that God is identified with cod), and that fish or goat meals in *Finnegans Wake* generally refer to a dismemberment and consuming of the old god, who suffers what Joyce nicely labels "mouth burial" (311:18 f.). Shem, living "among those rebels," is a "piscivore" (171:7 f.), that is, a fish-eater. The eating of fishes or goats, like a number of other actions in the book, is seen to be a ritual murder of God. As the fish to be consumed is the Eucharist, the goat is the animal of the followers of Dionysius. A number of other gods are similarly related to Joyce's playing with what we might call the fish-goat axis—Thor, Osiris, and Saturn, for instance. Prometheus (or Vulcan) is also associated with the goat (in this passage accusative of the Latin *hircus*), doing his dance at the edge of the volcano:

> *Quare hircum?* No answer. *Unde gentium fe . . . ?*
> No ah. Are you not danzzling on the age of a vulcano? Siar, I am deed.   [89:27 f.]

We see that there is no answer to the question "Where to with the goat?" But the question "from where in the world . . . ?" can be easily answered: the goat emerged from Noah's ark. A rather sophistical answer, perhaps because Joyce's playful inquiry into goathood brings him to the impenetrable mists of prehistory.

Joyce calls his book a "fishabed ghoatstory" (51:13), or a "tragoady thundersday" (5:13), a phrase that amalgamates the Greek *tragos* (goat), tragedy, goat, Thor's thunder, and Thursday (Thor's day). The book

103

is a "ghoatstory" in the sense that it recounts the falls of many men and gods now ghosts—and it is a riot or mob of women at a dionysiad, or goat-king's festival. HCE himself is a "goatservant" on display "for the triduum of Saturnalia" (97:33 f.). He is called Saturn (137:9).

The whole "ghoststory," dreamt by a fish "abed," seems to be assigned to "Thorkill's time" (51:16); that is, the story takes place during a god-killing period. "Bolt the door" reads as "bolt the thor" (279:n.); that is, Thor is killed and eaten. The bolt is also, of course, the thunderbolt of Thor, god of thunder, the sound of which, in Viconian theory, is the angry voice of God.

The gods and HCE are, in effect, repeatedly "assembled and asundered" (136:6 f.). Among the kings the rainbow girls take apart is "the goat king of Killorglin" (87:26). Again, Dionysius or Bacchus (perhaps Orpheus) are suggested. It is mainly to these two forms of "goat king" that God and HCE are related. HCE is clearly called "Dionysius" (70:36); he sits on a "bockstump" (70:17) after doing his dance. Drinking as well as dancing is involved here, since "Bock" is German for a kind of beer as well as for a male goat. HCE is said to have a "dhymful bock" (536:16). And God, the shepherd, lays down his gabardine cloak to sport with Bacchus: "Goteshoppard quits his gabhard cloke to sate with Becchus. Zumbock!" (276:12 f.).

This last word indicates another twist to the significance of God's goathood. "Zumbock" means not only "some buck" but also *zum Bock,* an exclamation like to the devil!—literally "to the goat." Furthermore, "Zumbock" means *Sündbock,* a scapegoat (*Sünde: sin*). The god sacrificed assumes, like Christ, the guilt of those who kill him. He is a "sindybuck" (412:35). The buck also appears in the place of the Holy Book in "So yelp your guilt and kitz the buck" (375:15 f.), which parallels the "So help her goat and kiss the bouc" passage already quoted. "Yelp your guilt" may be primarily an admonition to confess, but it also suggests helping your god (or guilt) by tickling, killing, or passing, the buck. The scapegoat consumes the record of the sinner's misdeeds, literally as well as ritualistically: "Scape the Goat, that gafr, ate the Suenders bible" (329:36 f.).

God's Human Failings

These vulgarizations of sacred beings and concepts seem to have a purpose; they illustrate a process that is dedicated, in the sentence following the passage "So in the names of the balder and of the sol and of the hollichrost . . ." (331:14 f.), "To the laetification of disgeneration by neuhumorisation of our kristianiasation" (331:31 f.). The passage shows that not only is degeneration made lighter and more joyful (Latin: *laetus*) by newly humorizing Christianity (with a glance at the city of Ibsen) but that part of Joyce's task is to illustrate how Christian customs and beliefs may be explicable by euhemerism; that is, explaining godly traits as the attributes of men who once lived on earth—on the assumption that pagan polytheism or Christian anthropomorphic notions of God had their genesis in the deification of dead heroes. Joyce is not only glossing Earwicker's creative functions by comparing them to divine functions; he is also explaining our ideas of God by euhemerizing God, showing that some of our ideas of God are explicable in terms of a common publican like Earwicker, just as the Homeric Odysseus is revealed through Bloom in *Ulysses*.

In bringing God nearer to earth, then, in approximating His qualities to our merely human intelligences, in investing Him with new testament love as well as old testament hate, we subject God to a "neuhumorisation," a Joycean brand of neohumanism, which will reveal the stultification of "old's code," the lowness of the creator, the unamiable aspects of "the fire of the lewd." God comes to mirror our own drives, to resemble a man like "joepeter" (426:21) or a euhemerized hero like Zeus:

"Besterfarther Zeuts, the Aged One, with all his wig-eared corollas, albedinous and oldbuoyant" (414:35 ff.).

"Albedo" is an index of the amount of light that the surface of a heavenly body reflects from a light source. Thus in "albedinous" the notion of a libidinous God, a bedridden old boy, is actually interpreted as an anthropomorphic notion; that is, our idea of God is a reflection of the source of those notions: ourselves. In this passage God–Zeus–Earwicker's crowns (Latin: *corolla*) glow only in man's imagination, only with the reflected glow of man's worship. Whatever glory these crowns may have, theirs is a conservative influence, an "oldbuoyant" influence. The anthropomorphic God becomes: "Mere man's mime: God has jest. The old order changeth and lasts like the first" (486:9 f.). The justice of God has become a jest, a passing order of justice no greater or more permanently valid than the justice of man himself.

God is a joke again and again in *Finnegans Wake*. "In God's name" becomes "in gogor's name, for gagar's sake" (102:8); God is "Dodd" (191:23), the mathematician and humorist Dodgson, or Lewis Carroll ("lewd's carol" in *Finnegans Wake*), whimsical creator of an Alice-in-Wonderland world. The reduction of God into a man of the people, a "mere man's mime," reveals him a "gag," as in "Gags be plebsed!" (485:10) or "thogged be thenked!" (487:7). A plebeian God is no longer a god, but a "gourd on puncheon" (373:20), punchdrunk on his pension, superannuated and *"foregotthened"* (345:34) by his creations. God's lust, then, which may once have had its creative function, lapses into his "imponence" (277:2). Finally, as we saw earlier, the ambiguity of "cod" allows for the meaning of "joke," along with the sacramental overtones of "fish."

God's Other Qualities

The vitality-impotence contradiction in the *Finnegans Wake* portrayals of God is only one of the many contradictions in the multitudinous insults applied to Him. But these contradictions are perhaps reasonable paradoxes, reasonable uncertainties in a portrait of the Almighty which explores a great many inadequacies. Like other "characters" in Joyce's works, finally God neither attracts nor repels us altogether. Joyce seems to suggest that in any event a legitimate attachment to God is now very difficult to achieve. God has been both pulled down to earth and withdrawn from our daily experience. At the same time that God is now a distant "farfar" (139:6) or "pharphar" (215:1), he is also dragged down from heaven to earth. He is like "J. B. Dunlop, the best tyrent of ourish times" (497:36 f.). The Irish absentee landlord is altogether a suitable parallel to the God of *Finnegans Wake:* God has become "His Diligence Majesty, our longdistance laird that likes creation" (457:23 f.). The rack rent He requires is "Rock rent" (221:32), certainly a reference to Maria Edgeworth's novel, *Castle Rackrent,* as well as to the rock of Peter's Church. The rent in question is prayer, as an earlier spoonerism suggests: "a gent who prayed his lent" (89:15).

Even the vigor of this landlord-deity undergoes a number of interesting permutations. The creator's medium, order, is advanced by vigorous action: "Ardor vigor forders order (614:9). "Forder" reflects two German words, *befördern* and *fördern,* meaning *to advance* and *to demand.* Joyce does not respect, it would seem, "applepine odrer" (287:16 f.), that is, neither ardor nor order. At times God becomes very soldierly, as in "To pass the grace for Gard sake!" (377:30 f.), and when he does he shares some of the unpleasantness of police and soldiery and some of the abuse heaped on them. In "may the mouther of guard have mastic on him!" (55:18 f.), or in "Guard place the town!" (356:34 f.) we also see a militant God, again in an unpleasant light, for the maxim that God made the country and man the town appears to be reversed here, and an evil normally attributed to man is assigned to "Guard." The same association is indicated in "Gothamm chic" (538:33). God, like HCE, is seen as modern man, a city-dweller, and in terms hardly applicable in the traditional city of God.

God's mercenariness is variously indicated, as in the exclamations "the Loyd insure her!" (413:5 f.) and "Delivver him, orelode!" (97:30 f.), and by the cry "God save Ireland" being turned into "Goldselforelump!" (613:1). Like HCE, he is an imperialist exploiter: "our hugest commercial emporialist, with his sons booing home from afar and his daughters bridling up at his side" (589:9 ff.). Joyce's abbreviation for "Let us praise the Lord" (Laus Deo) reads "Ls. De." (325:3), which looks somewhat like pounds, shillings, and pence in their abbreviated form. God shares this title with HCE, one of whose titles is "L.S.D." (107:2). This association of God with money is clearly supported by "Ad majorem l.s.d.! Divi gloriam" (418:4), in which the pounds, shillings, and pence are sandwiched into the Jesuit motto and liturgical echo, Laus Deo Semper. The whole world of the "Omniboss" (415:17) is regarded as God's wallet, bulging with "the opulence of his omnibox" (98:12 f.). The Ark of the Covenant becomes the "arc of his covethand" (321:27). A bishop is a "buyshop" (130:33). God's truth is commercially exploited by HCE, who lives "with an eye for the goods trooth" (107:16). And God himself shares in man's commercial lusts.

No wonder then that the Lord's prayer lives a life all its own in Finnegans Wake, and is our "pesternost" (596:10) or "patrecknockster" (81:28) or "Panther monster" (244:34) rather than the Paternoster. As the German "Vaterunser" it turns into the "fader huncher" (333:26), the "farternoiser" (530:36), and scores of other variations. One of the readings runs as follows: "Haar Faagher, wild heart in Homelan; Harrod's be the naun. Mine kinder come, mine wohl be won. There is nothing like leuther" (536:34 ff.). "His hungry will be done!" (411:11) and "dimdom done" (594:6) are of the same order. Twenty pages later we meet the same idea once more in "doominoom noonstroom" (613:3), and something similar in "Dies is Dorminus master" (609:28), in which day or God (deus) seems to be conquering night or sleep (the sleep is a permutation of "Dominus" or God). God's kingdom is one of doom or dimness, He is *His Murkesty* (175:23), and his "kingdom come" becomes "dimdom done" (594:6). God's truth is no longer unquestionable and sublime. It is "cock's troot" (113:12), "Colt's tooth!" (534:8), "Cold's sleuth!" (597:24), "goat's throat" (520:12), "goods trooth" (107:16), and so forth.

At two points the Paternoster indicates that God the Father is altogether passé. "In the name of the former and of the latter and of their holocaust. Allmen" (419:9 f.). God as creator is not denied here. He is still the "former," that is, maker, of the universe. The two meanings of "former" are more forcefuly emphasized at another place, where "father" is also meant: "Ouhr Former who erred in having down to gibbous disdag our darling breed" (530:36 f.). "Gibbous" is a triple-edged word here, meaning "give us," "the moon more than half full," and "apelike." The apelike breed God placed on earth, in other words, is accepted as His work, but judged to be a mistake. God's creation shows him to be a "Blonderboss" (442:27). We pray: "And gibos rest from the bosso!" (148:20 f.). Yet the mistake has its advantages; it is a "darling breed."

The Attraction of the Church

Shaun's pranks as a religious man—whether in his role as Jaun or as Kevin—and his corrosive comments on religious matters do not necessarily represent Joyce's definitive condemnation of the Church. The complex problem of Joyce's relation to the established church is difficult to illuminate with the ambiguous pieces of evidence we may glean from *Finnegans Wake*. We realize that criticism of an institution does not amount to its rejection, and that a "Rumnant Patholic" (611:24) or "roman pathoricks" (27:2) or "Robman Calvinic" (519:26) is not an anti-Catholic. The tendencies toward simultaneous acceptance and rejection are illustrated in the question James Joyce seems to pose himself: ". . . what say, our Jimmy the chapelgoer?—Who fears all masters!" (587:36). Does chapelgoing result from fear? It is not too clear whether chapelgoing and fear are effect and cause, or if this line is to be read as a statement of the paradox of homage and fear which may be entailed in any form of religiosity. However the authority of the Church is finally dealt with in *Finnegans Wake,* it is certain that where bare authority appears in the book it is never accepted graciously.

The reader of *Finnegans Wake* may take the largely one-sided battery of distortions directed against God and the Church seriously without necessarily being convinced that Joyce is here setting forth a definitive view of God and the universe. But if God really does have all these shortcomings, Joyce also attempts to explain why people nevertheless remain faithful to Him. Fear is the answer: fear that God's power is not altogether out of commission, and fear that we shall, after death, transfer to another kingdom more immediately under His jurisdiction. Whether we are Christians listening to the bell calling to Mass, or Mohammedans listening to the muezzin calling to prayer, we hear tidings of a dim world between Adam and our final doom: ". . . massgo bell, sixton clashcloshant, duominous and muezzatinties to commind the fitful: doom adimdim adoom adimadim" (552:23 ff.). The sexton rings the six-ton *cloche* to remind the faithful of doom.

The purport of this passage is more clearly enunciated in another passage which explains why men put themselves under the protection of God (in this case with characteristics borrowed from Noah and HCE:

". . . for the lure of his weal and the fear of his oppi-dumic, to his salon de espera in the keel of his kraal . . . afeerd he was a gunner but affaird to stay away" (497:14–17). Lured by the prosperity promised by God, or by His whip (weal in the sense of *welt* or *wale*), in awe of plagues on earth and of the unknown heavenly city (Latin: *oppidum*), man comes to the Church or into the keel of Noah's ark as cattle to the corral (*kraal* is a South African cattle enclosure), afraid God is a goner, or on the hunt, but finally afraid to reject this possible salvation.

8

James Joyce's Epic of Anarchy

MUCH OF *Finnegans Wake* is a denunciation of misuses of power; but the observation that power readily turns into tyranny does not mean that Joyce is a politically oriented writer—that he is an anarchist who wants to do away with all political sovereignties. A few political statements do appear in *Finnegans Wake,* and some of them reflect Joyce's feelings about authority; but we must not forget that the situations presented are largely human, not political; the book is a fiction, not a dissertation.

Political Comment in Finnegans Wake

Finnegans Wake is not altogether apolitical. Joyce warns us not to be too simple in reading his parables; he shows us that his brother pairs and dichotomized values may be susceptible to political interpretation. What first looks like the tickertape of an aesthetically-oriented production turns out to be shredded but redeemable banknotes of a rather different currency. The brother pair Caseous and Burrus, for instance, are obviously, among others, Cassius and, "obversely the revise of him," Brutus. Caseous is the "tyron" (163:9) of the pair; he is the Cavalier while Burrus is the Roundhead. Similarly, Jarl van Hoother and the prankquean are political opposites. And we may read with a political eye even such seemingly nonpolitical pieces as the letter dug up by the

112

hen and the passage about the girl falling off her "bi-sexycle" (115:16)—emerging into nubility from sex-ually bivalent preadolescence. The section itself, with its references to Freud, Jung, Lewis Carroll, and so forth, invites a psychologically intensive reading. Yet we are invited to read the whole as a political parable as well: ". . . Father Michael about this red time of the white terror equals the old regime and Margaret is the social revolution while cakes mean the party funds and dear thank you signifies national gratitude" (116: 7–10). And it is not too difficult to take the hint and interpret as political this "as human a little story as pa-per could well carry" (115:36). After all, most relation-ships have an exploiter-exploited content of some sort. The concept of the "sugar-daddy" suggested in this particular part of the book might be paralleled by im-perialist exploitation or benevolent paternalism or al-truistic missionary zeal, depending on one's point of view. A hint at the variety of possible interpretations is thrown out a few pages later when we are told that Margaret may have a meaning other than "social revo-lution," since Joyce has other tricks up his sleeve which we must not miss in reading his book: ". . . that (prob-ably local or personal) variant *maggers* for the more generally accepted *majesty* which is but a trifle and yet may quietly amuse . . ." (120:16 ff.). So Joyce invites us to interpret Margaret or Maggers as social revolution or as majesty; both readings are possible. With a snidely pseudoscholastic formality we are cautioned against any one-sided doctrinal interpretation, and told that too simple-minded a reading will not do justice to the author's intentions.

As a matter of fact, *Finnegans Wake* hardly supports any *particular* doctrines of "social revolution" or "maj-esty" or political party. Like Shem's room, it contains "tress clippings from right, lift, and cintrum" (183:29). We know that Joyce's socialism lacked overpowering conviction and energy. Marx's name occurs among a number of other evil influences of which Earwicker complains (365:20); and the attacker who testifies against HCE says "marx my word" (83:10) and is identified as a "cropatkin" (81:18), that is, an anarchist like the Russian Kropotkin. Later another assailant swears "by yon socialist sun" (524:25). And we find a reference to the Soviet (414:14) and the Kremlin (536:10), written as "krumlin," a reference to Dublin's Crumlin as well. Not very much more of a socialist nature appears in the book, except for the Viconian view of the class struggle.[1] Only the Bolshevik-Menshevik opposition is also toyed with a little. HCE's head is a "bulsheywigger's head" (70:21 f.). Of the revolutionary parties of Russia, Joyce prefers to identify himself with the lesser, less successful, moderate Mensheviks rather than with the Bolsheviks: "Man sicker at I ere bluffet konservative" (535:16 f.). The identification is made most clear in the sketch of Joyce's representative in *Finnegans Wake*, Shem: ". . . this Esuan Menschavik and the first till last alshemist wrote over every square inch of the only foolscap available, his own body" (185: 34 ff.). Shem, like the unportioned Esau or Menshevik party, completes his introversion by writing *to* himself and *on* himself, not an activity that a socialist would consider of much value.

Ibsen and Shaw

Joyce does draw some doctrinal support for his confrontation of the old conservative world from predecessors such as Swift, Sterne, Ibsen, and Shaw. Joyce's use of Ibsen and Shaw suggests a sympathy for their social and political views as well as a respect for their literary achievements.

In his own fashion of interpreting "Ibscenest nansence" (535:19) Joyce calls our attention to the nonconformist tendencies of some of Ibsen's plays: "For peers and gints, quaysirs and galleyliers, fresk letties from the say and stale headygabblers, gaingangers and dud-

der wagoners, pullars off societies and pushers on roth-
mere's homes" (540:22–25). Certainly the one truly
pervasive principle at work in all of Ibsen's plays—that
the community of man has as its chief duty the preserva-
cation of the individual's right to his separate development—was a principle Joyce sympathized with and
held to. Ibsen's revolutionary influence is granted such
power that the grandfathers—always signifying a weakening old order in *Finnegans Wake*—are warned to take
appropriate heed: "Shaw and Shea are lorning obsen
so hurgle up, gandfarder . . ." (378:24 f.).

Shaw himself crops up a few times in significant ways.
Joyce's treatment of *Pygmalion* seems to argue that a
flower girl, Shaw notwithstanding, could hardly be made
into a countess. He affirms, seemingly of Eliza: "The
eitch is in her blood, arrah!" (376:19) and three lines
later: "We could kiss him for that one, couddled we,
Huggins?" He asserts flatly that "You cannot make a
limousine lady out of a hillman minx" (376:3).

The Tyrant's Hat

Joyce's interest in the problem of obedience in a political context may also be indicated by his inclusion in
Finnegans Wake of a character such as William Tell.
The cap on the pole which William Tell was supposed
to salute appears repeatedly, as the "capapole" (622:30)
or "a perchypole with a loovahgloovah on it" (369:19).
But the arrogance of a Gessler is fated for a fall: "From
the hold of my capt in altitude till the mortification
that's my fate" (540:17 f.). It is true that a great many
hats and caps are waved in *Finnegans Wake,* few of them
obviously connected to the story of William Tell, and
they may have other functions than this symbolic one.
But considering the grasp of Joyce's memory and the
thoroughness with which other associations in the book
are belabored with variations, it seems unlikely that the
other caps in the portraits of dominant characters are
mentioned merely by chance. Jaun, for instance, in his

stormy address to his sister, declaims: "I'm the go-getter that'd make it pay like cash registers as sure as there's a pot on a pole" (451:4 f.). More specific talk of hats follows (452:4, 7). The first pleasures the tavern brawlers promise themselves after the deposition are to break Earwicker's bludgeon and drum and to confiscate his hat for a memento: "His bludgeon's bruk, his drum is tore. For spuds we'll keep the hat he wore" (372:25 f.). The pervasive irreverence to authority in *Finnegans Wake* does on occasion, we see, boil over into an active, revolutionary violence.

But on the whole Joyce's revolutionary tendencies are of a critical rather than of a violent nature. Perhaps he feels himself to be in the position of Skelton's Colin Clout (49:26), for whom criticism of the *status quo* is both more possible and convenient than violence. Joyce certainly scoffs at and fears a jingoist, whom he calls a "jingoobangoist" (364:32). Although Shaun accuses his Joyce-like brother Shem of being an incendiarist (426:2) and Guy Fawkes (425:23), the violence of Gunpowder Plot activity is turned off as "Tunpother, prison and plotch!" (364:26).

The Police

Joyce's feelings about violence and coercion also emerge in his rejection of policemen and soldiers. In both *Ulysses* and *Finnegans Wake* they are assigned a special status. In *Stephen Hero* the police are labeled "oppressors of the people," whereas they had simply been shown in uncomplimentary ways in *Dubliners*. In *Ulysses* Joyce made Carr, his enemy in Switzerland, a soldier. Joyce's feelings about the police run in an even stronger vein steadily through *Finnegans Wake*.

One of the ugly rumors brought up against HCE is that he is "reported to be friendly with the police" (137:18 f.). Generally the police represent a prying into private affairs, like the "Nazi priers" (375:18). The police are spies: ". . . the park's police peels peering by

for to weight down morrals from county bubblin"
(583:24 f.). But Dublin seems to bubble despite the
police. Even the morals-regulating function of God is
personified by a policeman: "Pay bearer, sure and sorry,
at foot of ohoho honest policist" (590:4 f.). This dis-
honest policeman shares in the deposition proclaimed
so decisively a few lines later: "His reignbolt's shot.
Never again!" (590:10). It is the final page of Book III
of *Finnegans Wake*. The police share in the final deposi-
tions of God, HCE, and Thor, lord of thunder.

What is wrong with the police? That their power is
based not on consent but on force, it would appear. For
the double significance of the term "policeforce" is emphasized in locutions such as "pentapolitan poleets-
furcers" (565:4) or "forced a policeman" (580:7). The
Heliopolitan constabulary" (530:16 f.) rely on the
"wordybook and the trunchein" (530:19). When guns
speak, their first words are an admonition in the
"Thou shalt not" style of the four guns, the four gospelers: ". . . never underrupt greatgrandgosterfosters!"
(368:4). Respect for military and police authorities,
like religious conformity, is one of Earwicker's rules of
thumb: "Mind the Monks and their grasps. Scrape your
souls. Commit no miracles. Postpone no bills. Respect
the uniform" (579:12 ff.).

The police achieve the disturbing effect of eliciting
unctuously pleasing behavior (is this autobiographical
revelation, perhaps?). When the police are out of the
way a man can "talk straight turkey":

> Let us now, weather, health, dangers, public or-
> ders and other circumstances permitting, or per-
> fectly convenient, if you police, after you, police-
> police, pardoning mein, ich beam so fresch, bey?
> drop this jiggerypokery and talk straight turkey
> meet to mate. . . . [113:23-26]

The police, in other words, enforce conventions of behavior which we would otherwise throw off.

But the "straight turkey" that follows is still a little

contaminated: "I am a worker, a tombstone mason, anxious to pleace averyburies and jully glad when Christmas comes his once ayear. You are a poorjoist, unctuous to polise nopebobbies . . ." (113:34 ff.). The "poorjoist" is willing to perjure himself, he is so anxious to please the "nope!"-saying bobbies (and nobodies). But he is also unctuous, and is identified as Joyce himself, "poorjoist," who cannot stand up to authority when face to face with it, "cannot smile noes from noes" (114:2) with the police, despite his own injunction to "learn to say nay!" (193:12).

The please-police antinomy inherent in "unctuous to polise," incidentally, reflects the persistent paradox in Joyce's work: the simultaneously pleasing and objectionable character of authority. In *A Portrait* the dean tries to convince Stephen to join the order by pointing to the "awful power" (p. 448) Stephen will then have. But "awful power" is not all allurement to Stephen, who chooses freedom for himself. Buck Mulligan in *Ulysses* contains in his personality a similar paradox: he is a charming tyrant, and he displays the exuberant confidence of one who swims with the tide, while Stephen plays foil to him, a dull outcast and insecure would-be artist. In *Finnegans Wake* policelike Shaun takes Buck Mulligan's role. Violence-meditating Shaun says: ". . . I have of coerce nothing in view to look forward at unless it is Swann and beating the blindquarters out of my oldfellow's orologium . . ." (410:2 ff.). It is exactly coercion that Shaun has in view; it is coercion that he has "to look forward at." His appeal is in part derived from his autocratic mannerisms, and he entertains us as no saint could, with an obstreperousness and wit which are fine to read about, but which would make life with him difficult indeed.

Finnegans Wake *as Apolitical*

The cure for the ills of the world inhabited by HCE (Humphrey Chimpden Earwicker, Here Comes Everybody, *et al.*) may be sought in political agitation. But a more local, that is, psychological rather than doctrinal, medicine is successfully and ubiquitously at work in the book: the ministrations of ALP (Anna Livia Plurabelle), the eternal feminine:

> Though the length of the land lies under liquidation (floote!) and there's nare a hairbrow nor an eyebush on this glaubrous phace of Herrschuft Whatarwelter she'll loan a vesta and hire some peat and sarch the shores her cockles to heat and she'll do all a turfwoman can to piff the business on. Paff. To puff the blaziness on. Poffpoff. And even if Humpty shell fall frumpty times as awkward again. . . . [12:7–13]

To paraphrase: the land is inundated by the flood (German: *Flut*) and the vegetation is swept off the credulous globular face of the world, a place of corrupt leadership (in German *glauben* means *believe, Herrschaft* means *mastery* or *leadership,* a *Schuft* is a *scoundrel,* *Welt* means *world,* and *Wetter* means *weather*). Nevertheless ALP will gather the remains of religion (the *Avesta* are the sacred writings of Zoroaster), clothing, fuel, and food and keep life going, even if man should fall again and again. The world of *Finnegans Wake* is one of recurring rise and fall, but also one that recognizes and values continuity.

So we must admit that, although *Finnegans Wake* treats the problems of the world from a highly organized, anti-authoritarian point of view, it is not a thesis that pushes a political sort of anti-action very far. If the book sticks to a thesis, it is rather a faith in man's endurance, a faith that goes hand in hand with the epic stance, which observes rather than bewails. This stance is coupled with another attitude, as in the foregoing passage about the resurrecting female, of acceptance—acceptance of affairs as they have been and are likely to be. This acceptance of the world, we must note, however, is not set in any discoverable teleological framework—we have acceptance of the *processes* of historical change, without a certain recognition of a *purpose* or end of historical change. As far as is readily discoverable from *Finnegans Wake*, Joyce injects no purposeful aim into his portrait of the universe. The world of the book, the nightmare of history, is "Willed without witting, whorled without aimed. Pappapassos, Mammamanet" (272:4 f.). That is, the world was willed into existence without wit; the orbits of the heavenly bodies are whorled, curved, without aim nor end. The father passes on, the mother remains (Latin: *manet*) to "puff the blaziness on."

This is one of the implications of the fortunate fall, the *felix culpa:* the fall is not final. That is the revolutionary's creed and hope. Good must emerge from each cataclysm. And it is a good that achieves a distribution among the generality: ". . . the evil what though it was willed might nevewtheless lead somehow on to good towawd the genewality" (523:2 ff.). Before the fall the generality are mere tools of the great: "If this was Hannibal's walk it was Hercules' work. And a hungried thousand of the unemancipated slaved the way" (81:3 f.). So the fall inevitably relieves as well as breaks. It brings a new good in the track of ruin. The "genewality" implies not only genuflection but also a new *Wahl* (German: *election*) on the part of the populace.

The Fall Not Tragic

The epic stance is not the only factor that undercuts the possibility of viewing this cyclical process as tragedy. If life really does go on, even though "Humpty shell fall frumpty times" over again, this also means that the falls of man are not tragic. Neither the personal nor the political fall is ever really quite complete—something respectable carries on as each age is fused to the next. Furthermore, if the recurring fall is inevitable, we have a third reason why it cannot be tragic: in the normal

120

sense of Western drama, the inevitable is not tragic, cannot be. The tragic by definition is avoidable. Perhaps this view helps explain why Joyce's book is true to its epic program by being neither nihilistic nor positively pessimistic. Joyce accepts the unavoidable with good grace. In a sense the view of history in *Finnegans Wake* is Hegelian: thesis conflicts with antithesis, and the resulting synthesis engenders a new antithesis, ad infinitum. The process is not criticized; it is simply the process of change.

Finally we must see that this eternal recurrence of cataclysm is not only displayed and accepted—it is accepted and approved. It is just as well, we are instructed, that every idol has feet of clay and will topple. HCE, for instance: ". . . his headwood it's ideal if his feet are bally clay" (136:33). His feet are on "bally clay"—that is, the shifting ground of a battlefield (Balaclava in the Crimea) or Dublin (according to P. W. Joyce,[2] its Gaelic name, *Baile-atha-Cliath* is pronounced Blaa-clee). In *Finnegans Wake* the idol with feet of clay, then, is the "ideal" structure. Idols, by definition, are meant to be toppled.

We must conclude that it is well that the cycles eternally recur. History never comes to a halt with a final Marxian synthesis so satisfactory that its antithesis is never engendered in its turn: we see the toppling of hero after hero, thesis after thesis. But this succession is not tragic because it is viewed from that epic distance that allows to all contrarieties some plausibility, and because it is inevitable, because it is just, and because the repeated downward plunges are relieved by a more profound continuity, "Mammamanet," the creative urge survives.

Obedience as Cause of the Fall

We must inquire then more closely why all this toppling is necessary. Exactly what is responsible for the Flood? Why did Adam and all his successors in their respective

Gardens of Eden fall? Joyce seems to toy with a number of notions without accepting any of them altogether. The accepted theory of how God brings about the fall of man, for instance, is somehow fundamental to *Finnegans Wake:* man, because of his own crime, is responsible for his fall. But this view is not accepted without reservations. In Milton's reading of the problem in *Paradise Lost* Adam's crime is pride, disobedience. God's wrath is called forth by man's villainy and lack of trust: namely, by his refusal to abide by God's command. Yet Joyce did not altogether accept such reasoning about man's fall from Eden as is found in Genesis and St. Augustine and Milton and Vico.

Joyce does not judge disobedience to be a detestable crime, but rather the opposite. Although he seems to see society with a marked bifurcation into ruler and ruled, government and people, crime in Joyce's history is more readily a function of ruler than of ruled. The ruler is responsible. We see this accusation in the long quotation on page 119 above; the flood is caused by the "Herrschuft," the scoundrel leaders. Not by the people. The people are responsible only insofar as they are part of the "glaubrous phace" of the weather—insofar, that is, as they are in a credulous phase and willing to agree to what is decided for them. Joyce fears but also respects power. For him the matter of fact is a "fatter of macht" (150:11). The father with might (German: *Macht*) gets to eat the bacon. Force is associated with the ruler, and force enables him to commit deeds impossible to lesser men. The great man's peace is an oppression by force: "sivispacem (Gaeltact for dungfork)" (87:14); the Pale within which the English lived in Ireland is associated with the most primitive violence: with the "ancient flash and crash habits of old Pales time ere beam slewed cable" (289:8 f.); here the God of thunder still rules a Palestine antedating Cain's slaughter of Abel. Political as well as churchly hegemony is held by unscrupulous forces, the violent force of the old Palestinian gods. The festive halls of Tara, ancient capital of Ireland, are based on the rule of the fist—they are "faustive halls" (74:9) (*Faust* is German for *fist*). Bishop Walsh (whose name rhymes with "belch" in Joyce's poem "Gas from a Burner") is called "old billfaust" (160:26 f.). Ruler, not ruled, has power. Ruler, not ruled, is in the position to commit great crime.

It is true that Stephen professes "scorn for the rabblement" (*Stephen Hero*, 122 f.), that democracy in *Finnegans Wake* is punned into "demoncracy" (167:25), and that representative government is "Impovernment of the booble by the bauble for the bubble" (273:6 f.). Yet even here the people are guilty only insofar as they are impoverished by their leaders. The only sort of leader for whom Joyce shows respect in *Finnegans Wake* is one like Buddha or Parnell who has a position by virtue of his capability but does not use his power to oppress those under him.

The fall of Parnell is a case in point. Parnell was not toppled so much by the Irish as by other political leaders, in England as well as Ireland, and by the church, which stirred up the people against Parnell. The people are only secondarily guilty by agreeing to or accepting his fall. This view of responsibility is that of modern apolitical man, whose connection with the circles that determine policy seems to the layman astronomically remote. Like the primitive who finds the king guilty when catastrophe strikes the land, this view tends to put blame on the more powerful of the dichotomy of ruler and ruled, not on the weaker. Consequently Joyce's interest in great men. It is true that Joyce often writes about the common man, about an advertising canvasser like Bloom or a pubkeeper like Earwicker; yet the *Finnegans Wake* view of the battles of the world, like Balaclava or Waterloo, is focused less on the soldiers than on the generals in charge. The responsibility for victory, the guilt for failure, is placed with leader rather than with led.

Joyce and Milton

And the responsibility is placed with God as well as with Adam. Joyce's treatment of the relation of ruler to ruled extends to his treatment of the fall of man. The theory is followed in Joyce's repeated use of Milton's *Paradise Lost*, which he puns into "Peredos Last" (610:34) and other variations. Like Milton's work, Joyce's is ostensibly about the cause of man's first disobedience and its effects. That Joyce considered his own work a remote parallel to Milton's is variously indicated.

We see it in the echo of the opening lines of Milton's poem: "Of manifest 'tis obedience and the. Flute!" (343:36). Joyce's work has the same subject at its center. The Dublin greens where the fall of HCE takes place include Phoenix Park and also "Milton's Park" (96:10), which refers to Dublin's Milltown Park in Rathmines as well as to the scene of Milton's epic, the garden of Eden. And in a passage in which the famous "twohangled warpon" (615:19) from "Lycidas" appears, *Paradise Lost* occurs as "paladays last" (615:25). Not only *paradise* and *palace* are included in "paladays." Since *pala* is Sanskrit for *guardian,* a term repeatedly applied to HCE, "paladays last" means "the last or lost days of the guardian." In other words, "paladays last" as the title of a book refers to the story of both Adam's and HCE's fall from paradise; it is another title of *Finnegans Wake.* Since HCE is Everygod as well as Everyman, the title also implies the last days of god.

If Joyce's work is, like Milton's, about the fall of man, this is also the subject of the "Mamafesta" of ALP, or of the productions of HCE and his son Shem.

Shem, for instance, is said to be writing on the loss of the garden of Eden: "swobbing broguen eeriesh myth brockendootsch, making his reporterage on Der Fall

Adams" (70:4 f.). In his broken Irish brogue, in other words, he is cleaning up, or exchanging, an eerie Irish myth in bits (German: *Broken*) of broken Dutch, reporting on the case (German: *Der Fall*) of Adam's fall. He is recasting the myth into his own terms.

Shem too conducts, among other literary studies, a "study with stolen fruit" (181:14 f.)—a reference to Shem's (and Joyce's) plagiarism. But "study with stolen fruit" also indicates that he, like his father and his double, his creator, is tinkering with the myth of Adam and Eve and their theft of the apple of God's supreme wisdom.

What Joyce puts emphasis on in his treatment of the fall is the benefits of the happy fall, St. Augustine's "felix culpa." Joyce expands the concept in scores of variations on the phrase. Joyce makes little or nothing, however, of the disobedience by which the fall was brought about according to Genesis and Milton's version of Genesis. Joyce finds Adam and Eve more pitiable than reprehensible. HCE, in his role as Adam, gets off lightly for his collusion with Eve. At worst he is the "Bloody old preadamite with his twohandled umberella!" (530:28 f.). (The "two-handed engine" from "Lycidas" again.) Joyce asks if Adam and Eve, like Pyramus and Thisbe, were not pitiable creatures, *Armen* (German: *the poor* or *miserable*): "a garthen of Odin and the lost paladays when all the eddams ended with aves. Armen?" (69:10 f.).

Adam and Eve are thought more sinned against than sinning. Thy are "our forced payrents" (576:27). That is, our first parents, and the first human beings to have a taste of what the later Irish "payrents" suffered under English absentee landlords. God is seen as such a landlord, a "longdistance laird that likes creation" (457:24). He is our "Accusative ahnsire! Damadam to infinities!" (19:30). God, an accusative, destructive answer to the riddle of creation, was a most aggressive sire of our ancestors (German: *Ahnen*). God provokes the destruction of man by planting the tree of "prohibitive pomefructs" (19:15) in Paradise. Man must accept the challenge and eat of the "painapple" prepared for him by his Creator. And for this sin of a moment, this falling into a prepared trap, which Joyce hardly considers a sin at all, God damns Adam and Eve, possibly for all eternity. So Joyce accuses God as well as man, extending, in effect, the doctrine of original sin to include leader as well as led, God as well as man.

Joyce labels Milton's formulation of the paradox of the fortunate fall a positive heresy: "O felicitous culpability, sweet bad cess to you for an archetypt!" (263:29 f.). This condemnation is sharpened by a marginal gloss: *"Hearasay in paradox lust."* That is, the paradox of the fortunate fall is heresy as well as hearsay. Joyce, then, accuses Milton of using an idea that Joyce himself shows no compunction in exploiting. Joyce objects to Milton's poem altogether, calling it a "falsemeaning adamelegy" (77:26). For Joyce the disobedience which brings about man's recurrent fall and revival is man's high calling rather than the fortunate-unfortunate cause of Christ's redemption of man. The disobedience to God's law supposedly responsible for the recurrent fall has not a word said against it in all of *Finnegans Wake*. If anything is responsible for man's ills it is too much obedience rather than a moment of disobedience thousands of years ago in the face of a tyrannous master. The book is dotted with exclamations calling for deposition or assassination of masters, of fathers, of kings; but Joyce never exhorts us to bow.

The final Joycean analysis of the fall rests on the inevitability of man's will leading to temporary mastery and subsequent destruction. The devil *must* tumble from his throne, Adam is *bound* to fall, the king *will* meet his preordained assassin. Where man's will operates he will find a wall, like Humpty Dumpty, from which to fall, as part of one of the Persse O'Reilly ballads reminds us:

> Cleftfoot from Hempal must tumpel, Blamefool
> Gardener's bound to fall;
> Broken Eggs will poursuive bitten Apples for where
> theirs is Will there's his Wall. . . .   [175:17–20]

It is not disobedience that is responsible for the fall;
rather it is the will to be up on the wall above the others.
Perhaps this is why the fall from heaven of Satan or
"Cleftfoot" in the above ballad makes more of a thump
in *Finnegans Wake* than does Adam's fall from grace.
Adam had no throne from which to fall, whereas Satan's
troubles derived from an argument concerning sovereignty and command over others. The comment that
follows the ballad makes a similar distinction in the
antithesis of Christ and Lucifer, each of whom gets his
appropriate reward on the "Grampupus is fallen down
but grinny sprids the boord" pattern: "O fortunous
casualitas! Lefty takes the cherubcake while Rights
cloves his hoof" (175:29 f.). The downtrodden one gets
the cake; the ambitious and self-aggrandising politician
must be toppled. So disobedience is not the primary
agent responsible for the fall of man. The fall is a built-
in feature of man's role in history, for the will to thrive
leads to the will to excel; success itself breeds its con-
sequent misfortune, its own peculiar seeds of destruction. Joyce's relish for the destruction suggests that his
work revives the medieval genre of which Boccaccio's
De Casibus Virorum Illustrium and Lydgate's *Fall of
Princes* are prime examples, except that Joyce's work,
rather than exhorting princes to virtue and moderation,
exhorts the downtrodden to rise against their oppressors.

The Exhortation to Disobey

Man's birthright, Joyce argues repeatedly in *Finnegans
Wake,* is to seek freedom from oppression, oppression of
any kind. A number of the most fervent appeals to the
Ibsen doctrine of individuality in *Finnegans Wake* do
not seem to be directed particularly at the bonds of
family, religion, or state. To Shem (and thus to Joyce)

Shaun writes: ". . . your birthwrong was, to fall in with Plan" (190:12). A few pages later a similar admonition appears: "Cease to be civil, learn to say nay!" (193:12).

Obedience, we gather, is as much a crime as unjustified command. The prankquean, for instance, is admirable in her defiance of the inhospitable lord, Jarl van Hoother. When this HCE-figure gives an order it is a filthy business we are to connect with ordure: "he ordurd" (23:4). When the jarl and the prankquean finally make peace we are told in a version of the Dublin motto: "Thus the hearsomeness of the burger felicitates the whole of the polis" (23:14 f.). That is, the obedient (German: *gehorsam*) citizen makes the police or government (Greek: *politeia*) happy. Or by an alternate reading: reconciliation with authority (obedience) is a form of congratulation (felicitation) for the police.

Joyce, we see makes disobedience to tyrants a virtue. "Flame at his fumbles but freeze on his fist" (269:16), we are told in a politico-erotic paragraph. The "but" is at first glance misleading, since the statements read on the political level are supplementary rather than contradictory: object to his errors, resist his coercion. As tyrant, HCE has his initials built into the cry, "Hang coersion everyhow!" which dictates his overthrow: "You can't impose on frayshouters like os. Every tub here spucks his own fat. Hang coersion everyhow! And smotthermock Gramm's laws!" (378:26 ff.). In the foregoing passage the customers in Earwicker's pub shout: they are shouters in the fray, freeshooters, the "os" or bone of society. Every tyrant like Butt (*tub* backward) who is a despot, a "*desprot slave wager*" (354:7), as he is called, spits (German: *spucken*) forth his own antagonist, Taff (*fat*). Power has in it, in other words, that which will bring about its own destruction. Coercion must be eradicated; even the old linguistic standbys like Grimm's law must be superseded.

In short, obedience is bad, insubordination is glorious. And this extends far beyond the field of merely political suppression. Joyce exclaims, in echo of the statement engraved on Parnell's monument marking one end of Dublin's O'Connell Street: "No mum has the rod to pud a stub to the lurch of amotion" (365:26 f.). Parnell's words were: "No man has the right to put a stop to the march of a nation." Joyce's version makes a more general, apolitical statement, claiming that the lurch of emotion too is immune to the tyrant's censure. A limit is set to the power of man (and woman too, since *man* is turned into *mum*) over man. Joyce claims for himself not only political and religious freedom but also a personal and artistic freedom. The oxymoron "the lurch of amotion" paradoxically suggests Joyce's own writing, the epiphanies of which capture emotion recollected in tranquillity and transform the motion of life into the stasis of art. Over that art too, no outside intervention is tolerable. Freedom is the first requisite, as Joyce himself tells us, "to satisfy his literary as well as his criminal aspirations" (49:16). Of all the kinds of dictation, Joyce certainly refuses dictation over his art, which is not to be "licensed and censered by our most picturesque prelates" (440:11). The artist must be his own "ink-bottle authority" (263:24). The hand of another guiding his own will not do.

9

A Rebel's Métier:
Comedy and Obscurity

WE HAVE SEEN how Joyce's anti-authoritarian attitudes
influenced his wordplay, in particular in his references
to fathers in general and to certain father figures in
literature, mythology, history, religion, and politics. It
remains to explore the way in which his attitude toward
authority contributes to the increasing difficulty of his
two comic works. For if there is one question to which
the Joyce enthusiast must be prepared to reply, it is the
question of why Joyce in his later works kicked over the
traces of conventional English so thoroughly and chose
to work in modes so inaccessible to the majority of readers.

One answer to this puzzle has been that modern fiction is often unconventional and difficult because literature in general, and comedy in particular, is naturally
iconoclastic, and has always been so, even if not always
so radically as in the last millennium. The writer's natural iconoclasm results in a refusal to use the old forms
and in an affection for the new, the untried, the difficult.
One shortcoming of this theory is that writers of the first
rank, Homer, Dante, and Chaucer included, seem not
so much to have rejected the old forms as to accept them
as the starting point for the fresh and the new. Theirs

was an affirmative rather than a merely negative action —a necessary shaping of new containers for the new material which needed to be contained. Furthermore, although Joyce also adopted startling methods to help him express his ideas, he exploited an unusual range of literary precedent, from Homer to the latest magazine fiction. He seems to have honored his predecessors, even if his use of them suggests a studied irreverence for the authority of tradition or precedent. Furthermore, Joyce's originality is partly borrowed plumage: he adopted stylistic devices certain to lead him down the path of obscurity, such as Dujardin's stream of consciousness for *Ulysses* and the dream language of nonsense verse and word games for *Finnegans Wake*. The simple theory that writers naturally tend to iconoclasm will not explain the violence of Joyce's break with and simultaneous reverence for tradition, nor the obscurity that resulted from his experiments with language.

A second explanation for the difficulties of Joyce has been the old argument that our world is really more complex than it once was. Modern writing like Joyce's reflects modern complexities. In fact, however, that complexity is largely myth. Too many earlier cultures, when examined in detail—even subliterate ones like that of the Inca—look as highly organized and involved as ours. And if we compare our culture to others removed from us not by time but by space, we find areas in Europe which have not yet achieved our supermarket culture, but it would be meaningless as well as presumptuous to call these "simpler" cultures. Life is not simplified by the absence of labor-saving devices, by daily visits to a baker, a butcher, a greengrocer, a dairy, and a confectioner; nor is it much relaxed by a fourteen-hour working day. Our literature, in fact, has not so much reflected the complexities of our lives as it has imposed the idea of complexity on our imaginations. We are all affected by twentieth-century technology, but few of us are truly concerned with it or touched by it. Life is in some ways simpler than it once was, in some ways less so. Modern writing reflects a change in kind, but hardly in degree.

Even if Joyce's world actually does make greater and more varied demands on its citizens than did Henry Fielding's on his, this will not explain the difference between a comic epic like *Tom Jones* and another like *Finnegans Wake*. And how much did Joyce's world become more complex between the time he wrote *A Portrait* and *Finnegans Wake?* H. C. Earwicker's world does not seem to demand more of him than Stephen Dedalus' world demanded of him. Yet the later book is immensely more difficult than the earlier.

A third explanation for Joyce's obscurity also fails to hold up under inspection: Edmund Wilson claims that *Finnegans Wake* is most obscure where it makes the most embarrassing revelations. Wilson's own example, the revelation of Earwicker's incestuous tendencies, is robbed of point by those short passages in which incest is more clearly indicated. For instance, the story of Honuphrius and Anita (pp. 572 f.), who are also Humphrey and Anna, is written in as conventional an English as anything in the book—in this instance the style happens to parody the involvements of Plautine comedy. Joyce's obscurity or originality is not that simple a function of the unacceptability of what he has to say.

If none of these three explanations satisfies the puzzled reader, a fourth may at least offer insights into the growing complexity of Joyce's work. As his work grew more difficult, it also became more original, and as it grew more original, it grew more comic. What I am suggesting is that the increasingly complicated nature of Joyce's work is understandable if we view him as a great comic writer, for the difficulties we encounter in Joyce are of the same kind as those displayed by other great comic writers, although different in degree. Comedy has often tended to present difficulties to the reader, to pile up paradox on paradox, as in Rabelais and Shakespeare and Sterne. This tendency shows in more recent comedy as well: in the paradoxes of Oscar Wilde, for instance, and in the work of Pirandello and Ionesco and Beckett. And often the more paradoxical and multilayered the statement, the funnier it is. The funniest speculations of a character such as Gully Jimson of Cary's *The Horse's Mouth* are the most paradoxical ones; the peak of hilarity in *Ulysses* probably occurs in the Oxen of the Sun episode, which is so difficult to comprehend that only the most learned exegesis can explain it in detail.[1]

Another factor contributing to the difficulty of so much comic writing is that it relies on references to current fashions and foibles which the transit of a few miles or years will make unintelligible to the average audience. This is why we often find Aristophanes and Shakespeare obscure in their comedies. Comedy likes to feed on the vulgar particularity of the present, but as present becomes past the reader speeds away from a sense of the past with ever-increasing velocity. The pace of increasing modernity generates a phenomenon for the critic which we might equate with the red shift discovered by the astronomer, the not-too-distant past hurtling away from him with ever-increasing vigor.

Transcriptions of the quotidian experience soon become obscure not only because today's slang and household gossip is forgotten tomorrow. A man's sense of the everyday is personal, individual, alogical. The everyday is a seemingly illogical concatenation of events, a chain of specific acts with a very particular flavor. Tragedy tends to ignore that flavor in preference for effects more sublime, but comedy conveys and exploits it. Good comedy, even within the frame of a neatly designed plot, becomes a tribute to the complexity and comparative incomprehensibility of human experience. Low as comedy may sink—to pun, farce, slapstick, cruelty, obscenity—it performs this serious function. With a laugh comedy readily digests what the intellect finds inexplicable. Comedy is often akin to poetry in this way, that it conveys as well as explains.

133

Furthermore, Joyce's comedy is verbal; it relies on wit. Wit requires an exercise of intellect on the part of the audience; it functions as an obstacle in the way of easy comprehension. Joyce's comedy is also unusually original, mixing what familiarity has taught us to understand and contemn with the utterly new, with the "terrible beauty" of the latest fad, the unprecedented surprise. That much-discussed obscurity for which Joyce is famous, therefore, stems also from the originality that great comic writers have in common, an originality that Joyce pursued with unusual vigor, partly for esthetic reasons, but also because he so keenly felt the unusability of the old ideas and styles unchanged. Laughter itself is a physical reaction to degraded values, as well as a tool for degrading values,[2] and is therefore the iconoclast's ideal weapon. That we cannot always exactly identify the target of the comedian's shafts does not make us laugh any the less.

Joyce's wit, probably because it mocks authority and is often hard to follow, is open to the objection that it is merely clever, an arrogant species of joking in which the author shows his own superiority at the expense of a maltreated reader. Of course this arrogance in wit is hardly peculiar to Joyce. In Wilde's *The Importance of Being Earnest,* for instance, the spectator is invited to admire the playwright's superiority and profundity. Unfortunately or not, Joyce also betrays such a presumption to superiority, and many a reader will resent it.

But like the comedy of Wilde, Joyce's comedy also contains a wealth of importance and meaning; his wit is more than merely clever. It is true that the difficulties of *Ulysses* have caused critics to call it a gigantic hoax. But the most thorough attempt to demonstrate that the whole book is a joke, albeit a respectable joke, is manifestly unconvincing.[3] Perhaps partly in response to attacks from various quarters, Joyce included in *Finnegans Wake* some rather grandiose, but not altogether

134

empty claims for the universality, the profundity, and the epic grandeur of his work, although he does poke a bit of fun at himself here and there for collecting "jests, jokes, jigs and jorums for the Wake" (221:26), and calls himself a mere "wordpainter" (87:13) and a "pucking Pugases" (231:21). But if his "noveletta" (87:23) is merely a "school for scamper" (80:34), it also claims to be a grand "epical forged cheque" (181:16), "piously forged" (182:2) for a demanding public. All of history from the Neanderthal man through the present to the cataclysms of the future is encompassed in this "meandertale" (18:22). The "nameless shamelessness" (182:14) of "quashed quotatoes" (183:22) adds up, finally, to absolutely everything: to a *"Pantojoke"* (71:18) of "mooxed metaphores" (70:32), to a "poly-gluttural" (117:13) "prepronominal *funferal*" (120:9 f.) in which the comedian-artist's "probiverbal" (60:32) "payrodicule" (70:6) is cradled in a Homeric nomen-clature—"nomanclatter" (147:21). Joyce's ideal insom-niac highbrow reader will appreciate the "farced epistol to the hibruws" (228:33 f.) and see the tears behind the comic mask.

The *Epistle to the Hebrews* is only one of the works on which Joyce seems to model his own, or perhaps one of those he thinks subsumed under his own production. *Finnegans Wake* as "scherzarade" (51:4) imitates *The Arabian Nights*, the "Aludin's Cove of our cagacity" (108:27 f.). Joyce compares his work to many of the great books of all time, such as the *Koran* and *The Book of the Dead*, as if to balance the playfulness of an other-wise farcical production. He also calls *Finnegans Wake* a mighty "nightynovel" (54:21) or "nightlife instru-ment" (150:33), a "reporterage" (70:5) on all the sins of man, a monolithic "onestone parable" (100:26 f.) or "radiooscillating epiepistle" (108:24). It is a repository of the world's arcane knowledge, a "vehicle of arcanisa-tion" (135:27), at the same time that it seeks to explain to its readers: "to explique to ones the significat of their exsystems" (148:17 f.)—existence defined in terms of worn-out systems ripe for replacement. In other words, Joyce tells us that in *Finnegans Wake* "punplays pass to ernest" (233:19 f.)—the puns are worth deciphering. The recalcitrant reader may object: "our undilligence has been plutherotested so enough of such porterblack lowneess, too base for printink!" (187:16 ff.). But the reader who considers his intelligence too much tested is castigated by Joyce for lack of diligence, or "undilligence."

Finnegans Wake thus claims for itself the title of a seriously intentioned scherzo. It makes fun of the high for the sake of the low, of the past for the sake of the future; it shreds up and ridicules the pretensions of the history books to show the texture of daily events which all men experience in common, and to throw light on the present and on times to come. Although Joyce's "heart, soul and spirit turn to pharaoph times, his love, faith and hope stick to futuerism" (129:36 f.). Ages to come are to be guided by his look at far-off, Pharoah days; for at its most serious, the book presents its readers with, ". . . a theory none too rectiline of the evoluation of human society and a testament of the rocks from all the dead unto some the living (73:31 ff.).

The originality of the artist, then, provides a "theory none too rectiline," a truth as well as a joke to make us laugh. Any moral work, *Dubliners* included ("a chapter in the moral history of my country"), seeks a modus vivendi for man, an interim pattern or set of goals tolerably acceptable while the ultimate quest is in progress. The moral pattern in *Dubliners* cannot lead to salvation, whatever the ultimate quest may uncover. With no worthy ends of their own to work toward, the inhabitants of that world are entrepreneurs at best: Lenehan, Mr. Duffy, Farrington and Mr. Alleyne, Maria's Alf, Mr. Tierney, Mrs. Mooney and her son Jack, Mrs. Kearney, Tom Kernan, even Gabriel Conroy. Their modus vivendi

136

reveals itself as a cracked sort of one-upmanship, success at which brands the entrepreneur on the treadmills of self-promotion as damned, as exploiter, as selfish cad. The comedy of a story such as "Grace" is sardonic and sordid indeed. What is sordid in the naturalistic slice of life is that its characters are frozen in wrong-headedness, in mistaken motives. Joyce's characters are egotistically grubbing on a small scale at the expense of other values, stated or implied. They are afflicted by a diseased and unrewarding paralysis in habitual gestures which can bring no respectable reward. Put the entrepreneur on the psychiatrist's couch, and you can only cure him of his nervousness by getting him to give up the game, getting him to stop caring whether he is one up or not. This is the lesson Gabriel learns, at least momentarily: throw away certain values in your present life the pursuit of which cuts you off from other and more essential values. Michael Furey, never one up, turns out to have been one up on Gabriel. Dead, he has the last laugh. He had the love of a woman whose love Gabriel had not questioned, and had hardly missed.

Of the four chief works of fiction Joyce wrote, *Dubliners* is the most negative. The "cracked looking-glass" of these stories reflects the miasma only, not the way out, and what comedy the book contains is painful and unconstructive. In *A Portrait* some alternatives are mirrored as well. Religious renunciation of one-upmanship takes over from the ideal of worldly success. If at first you don't succeed, Joyce is saying here, give up the game and say that henceforth you will be one up on yourself rather than on other people, which sounds noble enough. But later the bird-girl epiphany on the beach converts Stephen to a more complex sort of renunciation.

The dark sarcasms of a more mature Stephen are the sardonic thrusts of the "outcast from life's feast," who resolves to create an even better feast in the smithy of his creative soul. But he does not altogether renounce renunciation. He resolves on a renunciation of authority in general, and more particularly, of community, family, perhaps of love itself (which can establish an uncomfortable authority of its own). The esthetic ideal is that of the secular saint, whose goal is dissociation, the goal Buddhists recognize as a purification of the self, a goal called "dying to the world" in Christian mysticism. (Dissociation is also a necessary attitude for the writer who is to produce effective comedy, that is, look at his subject not from inside but at arm's length.) Stephen's rather humorless dissociation is finally more Bohemian or Beatnik than Christian. Stephen (or Joyce?) renounces subservience to the usual dicta of society— Gerty MacDowell's "Society with a big ess"—without renouncing the right to suck its most succulent herbs and berries, such as seven-course dinners in the best restaurants. This is to be one up indeed.

The new modus vivendi we see explored in *A Portrait* and in *Ulysses* assumes that the old rules are rubbish. Simply to pronounce them in a certain way is to make your audience laugh. If any ambition is to be valued, it is to dissociate from the authority of inconvenient superstitions, such as the abject acceptance of external discipline, and to turn to the pleasures of excelling in the more personal and individual disciplines of art and liberty, in which it is difficult to succeed, but easy to be one up. The artist, at least in his own head, gets at arm's length from the world and learns to laugh at it, at the same time that he still takes part in the picnic. Thus Joyce, in the process of detachment, developed a stance of amused attachment which never left him. So we cannot claim either that Joyce simply rejected or simply accepted his world. His reaction is more complex than that of either acceptance or rejection; it is rather a comic ambivalence which thrives on a juxtaposition of opposites, on a tension which may not be resolved.

This comic ambivalence did not spring into being all at once. The early works are both more serious and straightforward than the later ones, just as they tend to a relatively simple identification of the enemy to be rejected. To come to grips with an inimical and nasty world, the writer brings the beloved enemy nearer into focus for himself, and therefore for his readers. He is not so detached an observer as he pretends to be, for in *Dubliners* Joyce sought to identify the poisons that he wished purged from the body of Ireland. In the test-tube of art the substance that we hope to eliminate from our blood is identified. Such an attitude makes for consistent and comprehensible characters—caricatures at odds with others rather than with themselves. Many of the characters of the early stories are puppets illustrating different aspects of their author, rather than self-contradictory and conglomerate human beings like Bloom and Earwicker. Even Gabriel Conroy is a grotesque and a caricature compared to Earwicker, who encompasses views and qualities incompatible with one another.

In *Dubliners* and *Exiles* a few conflicting characteristics are apportioned in traditional fashion between different characters. In *Exiles* juxtapositions are all too clear. But in *A Portrait* incompatible roles came to be apportioned among various developmental stages of a single person, who is several different people at successive stages, as we might expect in a novel rather than a short story. In *Ulysses* the chief characters are more thoroughly self-contradictory, and therefore strike us as more fully realized and rounded people. In *Finnegans Wake* the simultaneity of opposites is a docrtine fully imposed on the language as well as on the characters, so that the words themselves live and change and fuse with each other. They comment on other incarnations of themselves, as, for instance, "joepeter's" (426:21) and "shoepisser pluvious" (451:36) comment on Jupiter Pluvious. Like the warring twins everywhere in the book, they are often incompatible with forms to which they are most similar (St. Patrick and "Mr. Trickpat" [487:23]). The language of *Finnegans Wake* deftly locks opposites into the embrace of a single word ("betrue" [459:20] means "betray" in the context), suggesting the equivalence of opposites in hundreds of comic nonce-words, "any way words all in one soluble." Joyce's words are forged (in several senses) by an "ambitrickster" who cannot blame or praise without blaming and praising all at once. And the doctrine of the "coincidance of . . . contraries" (49:36) for which Joyce leaned on Nicholas of Cusa also defines humor: a consciousness of juxtaposed incompatibles.

Joyce's comedy of incompatibles must not obliterate his general drift: his egoism as well as his idealism forces him to pity servitude and to slash at authority. Like Skelton's Colin Clout, Joyce uses language as his weapon of attack, for language, unlike action, serves to mask and manipulate feelings as well as to express them. Language is safer, more controllable than action, which besmirches the truths it seeks to embody, as we learn from Shakespeare's *Troilus*. And to revolt in words rather than in fact has the additional advantage that failure will not prove fatal. Joyce likes to poke fun at the world as a puppy enjoys mauling his master's slipper— he enjoys a vicarious destruction of untouchable might. And the further Joyce moves from reality the more brutal he can afford to be. The revolutionary proverbs in *Finnegans Wake*, such as "teak off that wise head!" (607:3), "Tyrants, regicide is too good for you!" (162:1), and "Synamite is too good for them" (494:33), are all "probiverbal" (60:32). That is, the word is a probe only (in German a "Probe" or dress-rehearsal for action), not the real thing. As Joyce says, his "war is in words" (98:34 f.). Or: "to put it all the more plumbsily. The speechform is a mere sorrogate" (149:28 f.). Words provide an avenue for the escape of pain, and they act as surrogates for deeds.

Language has another advantage over action: it can be rescinded in case of error. It is the natural instrument for the champion who is not quite sure he likes the lady he defends. Joyce himself expressed such an uncertainty in one of his many defenses of his last book's obscurity: "You will say it is most unenglish and I shall hope to hear that you will not be wrong about it. But I further, feeling a bit husky in my truths" (160:22 ff.). Absolute certainty, insofar as it exists at all, is necessary to deeds but not to words. To the writer, especially a native of "Doubtlynn" (248:7), absolute certainty is hardly more necessary than it is desirable; the writer will not fail for feeling a bit uncertain, "a bit husky" in his truths— husky in the sense of *hoarse* as well as *strong*. At one point in *Finnegans Wake* Joyce suggests that the writer (here it is Shem) ought not to set himself up too high: he must "pray for the loss of selfrespect" in order to do his instructive work; his scandalizing song is fed by certain well-defined uncertainties:

> . . . you have become of twosome twiminds forenenst gods, hidden and discovered, nay, condemned fool, anarch, egoarch, hiresiarch, you have reared your disunited kingdom on the vacuum of your own most intensely doubtful soul. Do you hold yourself then for some god in the manger, Shehohem, that you will neither serve not let serve, pray nor let pray? And here, pay the piety, must I too nerve myself to pray for the loss of selfrespect to equip me for the horrible necessity of scandalisang. . . . [188:14–22]

Again we note the conflicting or supplementary functions of priest and devil. The piper that the anarchical fool must pay in "pay the piety" is the tradition he denies— to sing the "scandal-I-sang" is the "horrible necessity" enjoined on the writer. Impiety is a duty implicit in his role. In effect, like the devil, he serves whether he wants to serve or no.

Only a Shaun-like speaker, a humorless go-getter, can claim his word unalterable, can believe he is not a bit hoarse or "husky" in his truths: "My unchanging Word is sacred. The word is my Wife, to expose and expound, to vend and to velnerate . . ." (167:28 ff.). It is true that Joyce himself may have thought that the word was his peculiar domain. But he could only call his own word sacred in the realization that no word, or perhaps every word, is sacred; the theory that words are sacred and unchanging is rendered ridiculous by the context of the passage. It is only this same Shaunish speaker who can say *"Ubi lingua nuncupassit, ibi fas!"*

"Where the language spoke, there is law!" is a most un-Joycean cry. For *Finnegans Wake* is a "sotisfic-tion" (161:2) or "benefiction" (185:3) or "cruelfiction" (192:19)—in context, satisfaction, benediction, and crucifixion—but always a fiction, never a law-giving instrument, always word, not act. Whether priest or devil, authority or rebel, Joyce creates in his dark comedies a world distinguished by the very fact of being non-real, provisional, and thus at its most brutally negative still a social act of exploration, a constructive rather than destructive statement.

Notes

CHAPTER 1.

[1] Louise Bogan, "Approaching Ur," *The Nation,* August 19, 1944.
[2] The following abbreviations and editions of Joyce's works are used:

    SH   *Stephen Hero*. London: Jonathan Cape, 1950.
    D   *Dubliners*. In *The Portable James Joyce*. New York: Viking Press, 1949.
    E   *Exiles*. In *The Portable James Joyce*. New York: Viking Press, 1949.
    U   *Ulysses*. New York: Random House, 1946.
    FW   *Finnegans Wake*. New York: Viking Press, 1947.

CHAPTER 2.

[1] Unless a different book is indicated, in this chapter and the next the page numbers in parentheses refer to the Modern Library edition of *Ulysses*.
[2] Marvin Magalaner, "James Mangan and Joyce's Dedalus Family," *Philological Quarterly,* XXXI (1952), 363–371.
[3] Arnold Kettle has claimed that Bloom's lack of heroism mars *Ulysses* rather seriously. *An introduction to the English Novel* (London, 1953), II, 148.
[4] Elizabeth Mignon, *Crabbed Age and Youth*. Durham, N.C., 1947.
[5] D. H. Lawrence, *Studies in Classic American Literature* (New York, 1953), p. 14.
[6] Adaline Glasheen points out that the Roman took his oath this way (personal communication).

CHAPTER 3.

[1] Stuart Gilbert, in his *James Joyce's Ulysses* (New York: Vintage Books, 1952), p. 255, suggests such a connection.

CHAPTER 4.

[1] J. S. Atherton, in *The Books at the Wake* (London, 1959), pp. 31 and 187, also finds such a theory of what we might term originator's sin at work in *Finnegans Wake.*

[2] For the Dublin associations of the name of Foster, see Vivian Mercier, "In the Wake of Fianna," in *A James Joyce Miscellany,* 3d series, ed. Marvin Magalaner (New York, 1962), p. 233.

CHAPTER 5.

[1] This use of *lobster* is one of many details for which I am indebted to Adaline Glasheen. The reference to the monster-lobster blunder of Thomas Sheridan in Dublin's Smock Alley Theater was located by Fritz Senn: *A Wake Newslitter,* 2 (April, 1962), 5.

[2] James Campbell and Henry Morton Robinson, *A Skeleton Key to Finnegans Wake* (New York, 1944), p. 258, n. 1.

CHAPTER 6.

[1] For a full reading of this passage, showing its relation to "Ivy Day in the Committee Room," the death of Parnell on the 6th of October, and J. F. Byrne's activity as financial editor of a newspaper, see Ruth von Phul, "Shaun in Brooklyn," *The Analyst,* XVI, 12.

[2] "Finnegans Wake and the Girls from Boston, Mass.," *Hudson Review,* VII (1954), 89–96.

[3] "*Finnegans Wake:* The Gist of the Pantomime," *Accent* (Winter, 1955), p. 23.

[4] P. W. Joyce, *Social History of Ancient Ireland* (2d ed.; Dublin, 1908), p. 23.

CHAPTER 8.

[1] See the entry under "Hosty" in Adaline Glasheen's *A Second Census of Finnegans Wake* (Evanston, Ill., 1963), p. 118.

[2] P. W. Joyce, *Social History of Ancient Ireland* (2d ed.; Dublin, 1908), p. 23.

CHAPTER 9.

[1] See, for instance, Daniel Weiss, "The End of the Oxen of the Sun," *The Analyst,* IX.

[2] Alfred Stern, "Why Do We Laugh and Cry?" in *Frontiers in Science* (New York, 1958), p. 295.

[3] Josef Baake, *Das Riesenscherzbuch Ulysses.* Bonn, 1937.

DATE DUE